Jacob's Ladder

from the Service book of St Aethelwold

It is the end of the world. Jesus is coming back. The clouds are all fiery, and round him are his angels carrying his cross, the spear which pierced his side, the sponge he was offered to drink from. They are the things which were used when he died for us. In his own hands he carries a book. I hope all our names are written in it!

JACOB'S LADDER

a Bible Picture Book
from Anglo-Saxon
and
12th Century English MSS

by

NICOLETE GRAY

FABER AND FABER
24 Russell Square
London

1949

First published in mcmxlix
by Faber and Faber Limited
24 Russell Square London W.C.1
Printed in Great Britain by
R. MacLehose and Company Limited
The University Press Glasgow

For
EDMUND

Foreword

This book is made up of a selection of drawings and miniatures from Anglo-Saxon and twelfth-century English manuscripts. It was made with two objects, which as I worked I found to coincide. I wanted to make a book of illustrations through which to teach children about the Bible. There are many books with beautiful pictures of Christian subjects, but very few which really illustrate the Bible, so often it is the same subject over and over again. I wanted to present a coherent story. But as I came to choose my pictures I found that I wanted also to understand what the artist meant in his treatment and his choice of subject. I have tried in my brief text to keep within his mind, not to attach to the pictures any meaning which would have been foreign to his intention. For his faith is mine and his intention I believe mine too; studying his work has immensely enriched my understanding, enlarged, but not altered my original purpose.

Between the mind of the Anglo-Saxon artist and that of his twelfth-century successor there are differences into which I have not attempted to enter; but all these artists illustrate the Bible in a way totally different from the Renaissance and post-Renaissance artists with whose interpretations we are so much more familiar. To them the Bible stories are not significant as mere events in time, nor as evoking personal emotional experiences, but as the sequence of God's revelation to man. The Old Testament only became fully comprehensible when it had been illuminated by the New Testament, when fulfilment showed that God had made his people prophesy not only directly in works, but indirectly by enacting in their lives over and over again allegories of the transcendent events of history, the Incarnation and the Redemption. For my interpretation of the incidents illustrated, I have sought only in sources prior to the manuscripts used, that is in the traditional exegesis of the Fathers of the Church, particularly St Augustine. I have seldom quoted their words, but every interpretation suggested is intended to be derived from St Paul, or from their commentaries. References are given under the list of plates at the end of the book.

It may seem perhaps that the allegorical conception of the Bible is too difficult for children. But surely it appeals to just that instinct which leads children to seek knowledge and expression through make-believe and play-acting? What is an allegory but a play where everyone knows that the actors represent something like, but other than themselves? We laboriously impress on our children the idea that historical and scientific knowledge is more real than the symbolic knowledge which they naturally accept. Are we really right?

[9]

In my choice of miniatures I have included pages from almost all the most notable manuscripts of the period now in England. I have, however, sought rather for sensibility in the treatment of the subject than for magnificence of design. I have in particular been fascinated by the extraordinary sense of spirituality of the Anglo-Saxon artists. They seem able to make each figure they draw express a soul, meeting other souls. My selection of manuscripts has been based on the fundamental work of Dr E. G. Millar's *English Illuminated MSS.* (1926), to which I would refer readers wishing for further information.[1] References are given to a few more recent articles. Quotations from the Bible are, in the Old Testament, partly from the Authorised Version, partly from the Douai Version; in the New Testament from Mgr Knox's translation. I have everywhere tried to keep close to the Vulgate, the text used in all the manuscripts except the Anglo-Saxon Psalter, Harley 603. Quotations have of necessity had to be drastically condensed and are intended to lead readers to the Bible narrative to which references are given in the list of plates at the end of the book. In cases where they differ, the first reference is to the Vulgate, that in brackets to the Authorised Version.

The translations from the Anglo-Saxon of the Junius manuscript have been specially made by Miss Christine Brooke Rose. They are not exact translations, since the narrative had to be immensely condensed, and the sophisticated and allusive vocabulary and construction simplified, to make them readable by children. But we hope that these sacrifices may have made accessible the spirit of the original, its naïveté and its grandeur. The lines from the *Dream of the Rood* are taken by permission of the Clarendon Press from Mr Gavin Bone's translation. For leave to quote from Mgr Knox's translations I have to thank his Eminence the Cardinal Archbishop of Westminster and Messrs. Burns, Oates and Washbourne.

I gratefully acknowledge the kindness of the owners who have allowed me to reproduce from the manuscripts in their possession; The Chatsworth Estates Company, the Bodleian Library, the British Museum, His Grace the Archbishop of Canterbury, Glasgow University Library, Corpus Christi College Cambridge, Trinity College Cambridge, the Dean and Chapter of Winchester Cathedral, and Pembroke College Cambridge. I owe a special debt to the staff of the Department of MSS. in the British Museum where most of the work for this book was done.

[1] More recent general works are T. D. Kendrick, *Late Saxon and Viking Art,* 1949; F. Wormald *English Illumination in the XII Century,* Journal of the British Archeological Association, 1943.

Jacob's Ladder

I

This is a picture of a story about the unicorn. The unicorn was the fleetest creature in all the world. No one could catch him. Then the hunters heard of a way. They were told to find a virgin; if she were in the wood the unicorn would come to her and allow himself to be caught. There she is sitting on a little hill in the wood and the unicorn has come into her arms and is looking up at her lovingly. He does not seem to mind the wounds the cruel hunters are giving him.

Why should this story be in a book about the Bible? Because it has a hidden meaning. The unicorn is really our Lord. No man on earth could have caught him or hurt him if he had stayed as God in heaven, but he loved the virgin. She is his church, or one can think of her too as any soul, yours or mine, which wants to belong to God. For love of her he became a man and allowed wicked people to hurt and kill him.

I have begun with this picture because many of the others in this book are like it. The artists have drawn Noah, perhaps, in the ark, or Abraham about to sacrifice Isaac, and their work is an illustration of the story as it is in the Bible. But they also had in their minds the hidden meanings of those stories. Our Lord when he came taught the people in parables. We do not understand all its meaning the first time we hear a parable; the more we learn about God, the more meaning we find. In the same way, before he came, God prepared his people with stories. Many of the stories he made them act in their lives like the sacrifice of Isaac, or Jonah and the whale. Only after he had come and lived his life as a man did the meaning of the stories become clear, and the reason why God had asked his servants and his prophets to behave as they did. The great Fathers of the Church, like St Ambrose, St Jerome, St Augustine, St Gregory, wrote commentaries on the Bible explaining all these meanings and I have tried to explain some in this book, partly because they explain the pictures, partly to give you a little idea of how rich the Bible is. It is like a great country full of palaces and rivers and forests, and you need not just look at the outside, you can go in and find all sorts of wonders you did not imagine, and wherever you go you will keep finding God.

from the Book of Beasts at Oxford

II

Now let us begin at the beginning. In the beginning was God, who had no beginning. This is a picture of God. It is one of the first pictures ever made of the Trinity. How hard it is to represent something which we cannot understand. But I think this picture does make it easier to understand. It is rather dark and difficult to make out; it is probably unfinished, but that is right. We cannot see God clearly yet, but only darkly, as in a glass; if the picture were clear and finished it would not be true, would it? I think this artist must have prayed a long time, and his picture is really true, an inkling of God. We can see, inside the great halo, God the Father sitting on his throne. On his knee sits his Son. How close together they sit! As if they were part of one another! As if the Son were the Father's own knowledge of himself, his Word about himself, as St John calls our Lord. Perhaps it is to show that he is the Word that the Son has a great scroll of paper going over his shoulders. Look, how the Father and the Son love one another! Their love is so great it is alive, it is the Holy Ghost, you can see him in the form of a dove, as he appeared at our Lord's baptism, standing on the arm of the Son, so close to them both that he shares all their thoughts. They are the Lover and the Loved One, and their Love; they are so complete to one another within the great circle of the O which encloses them, that they are one.

But though God is so complete in his Trinity and needs nothing, he made the angels and he made us so that we might have some of his happiness too. Look, they are holding in their hands the great ball of the world, how small it is!

from the Anglo-Saxon Psalm Picture Book

III

Before he created the world God made the angels. The next picture is about the fall of the rebel angels. The Bible is chiefly concerned with the history of men so this, which happened before they were created, is only mentioned there by the way, though our Lord told his apostles how he watched 'While Satan was cast down like a lightning flash from heaven'.

So I am going to tell you the story in the words of the Anglo-Saxon poem, of which this drawing is an illustration. Only I have had to shorten it a very great deal; it is a long poem which goes on to translate most of Genesis and Exodus. It is a very free translation but actually the first English version of the Bible. Now we cannot understand the Anglo-Saxon, so I have had it translated into modern English for you.

The Holy Lord God had created with his own hands ten orders of angels, whom he trusted well. They had joy and music and bright happiness. Great was their glory! They knew no sin but lived in peace for ever with their Prince. One of them He had made so beautiful, so mighty in his thought and let him grow so great that he stood next highest to Him in the heavenly kingdom, so fair and radiant that he was like to the bright stars. There he is, the tall figure at the top of the picture, in the middle. *Lucifer should have praised his Lord and thanked him for the gifts he had poured upon him in that light. But instead he turned to a worse thing, he stirred up strife against the most high ruler of heaven, who sits on the holy throne.*

Look, he is talking to the other angels; some are offering him their crowns already. This is what he is saying: '*Why should I serve? I can with my hands work as many wonders. I have great power to prepare a goodlier throne, higher in heaven. Why should I wait upon His favour and bow to Him with such homage? I will be God as well as He! Strong companions stand by me, who will not fail me in the fight! They have chosen me for their leader! I can be their Lord, rule in this kingdom! I will be His servant no longer!*' There is the great throne Lucifer wants for himself, and there on the line below he is giving out palms to his followers. They seem to think that the battle is won already!

Then Almighty God heard it all. How His angel had begun to raise himself and to speak foolish words against His Lord. Then the High Ruler of Heaven became angry, and threw Lucifer from his high throne. There is God throwing his terrible spears. *He rejected him from His favour and hurled him into hell, to the deep valleys, where he became the devil, the fiend with all his companions. They fell out of heaven for three days and nights, and because they would not honour His deed and word Almighty God set them joyless beneath the earth, in the murky hell.* There is Lucifer falling, and bits of his throne, its roof, and its grand cushion falling with him. He still looks very beautiful but right at the bottom of the picture he has reached hell

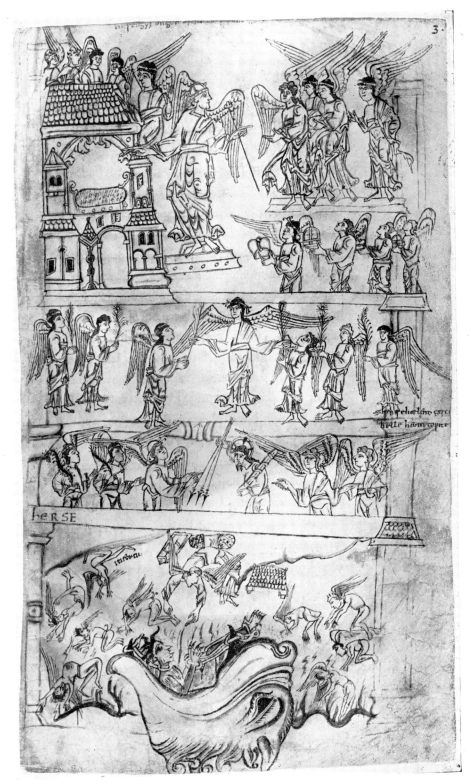

from the Anglo-Saxon Poetry Book

and is chained at its mouth. He is ugly now like the other angels who are falling all around, and his name has changed from Lucifer to Satan. The artist has drawn the mouth of hell like the mouth of a great monster. We pray in masses for the dead, that they may be saved from the mouth of the lion, and from the deep pit.

IV

*T*hen there was as before true peace in heaven. The Prince with all his glorious bands were in harmony. Strife had sprung away from among the angels now that the warriors, bereft of light, had departed. And widely throughout God's kingdom there remained behind them great thrones, radiant and rich in wondrous powers with none to sit on them, empty after the accursed spirits had departed to their exile and prison.

Then our Lord resolved in His mind to establish once again a glorious creation, noble thrones for a better band, now that the boastful fiends had departed. Therefore the Holy God willed that the earth and the sky and the wide water and earthly creatures, should be established under heaven's embrace. He decided to make people to fill up the empty places in heaven. Those wonderful thrones are for us!

This picture is of God creating the world. Nothing had yet been created here save the dark shadow, which lay sunk and dim, remote from God, empty and useless. First the eternal Lord raised up the firmament, and made it firm with His might. On the earth there was yet no green grass, for the ocean covered it, a black eternal night, wide and broad in dark waves. Then the spirit of heaven's guardian was carried wondrous bright and swift over the world, and the ruler of glories separated the light from the darkness over the waters; by the Lord's word light was first named day, and God saw the dark shadow sink away throughout the wide land. There is God sitting on the arch of the firmament; that is the great arch of the sky above the world. Below are the waters which still cover the earth, there is the Spirit of God moving upon the face of the waters. Above is another angel pouring out light upon the world. Can you not imagine as you look at the picture how clear and bright and pure that light is, touching for the very first time that wide sea; and how still it is! Only God is there; it reminds one of the morning of the resurrection, in the early light, when only God saw, and new life came to the world which was old then.

There is a lovely story told about the origin of this poem by the Venerable Bede. There was a poor man called Caedmon who was very bad at singing and inventing songs. One day he went to a party and everyone in turn was

God made the World

from the Anglo-Saxon Poetry Book

asked to play and sing. When he saw his turn coming he slipped out to the stable where he had to take care of the horses that night, and went to sleep. In his sleep someone called him, 'Caedmon, sing some song to me.' He answered, 'I cannot sing, that is the reason why I left the entertainment and retired to this place, because I could not sing.' The other answered, 'However, you shall sing.' 'What shall I sing?' 'Sing the beginning of created beings.' Bede tells us that after this Caedmon was able to write wonderful poetry, that he sang of the creation of the world, the origin of man, all the history of Genesis, and much more. The poetry which we have in our manuscript is probably not actually written by Caedmon, but whoever wrote it must have known his poem and probably copied it quite closely.

V

The next picture is from a very different book, a book about animals, made nearly two hundred years later than the Anglo-Saxon poetry book. It is the same book that the Unicorn picture (Pl. I) came from. Here it shows us the creation of the animals.

God had made the dry land, the grass and trees and plants. He had made the sun and the moon and the stars, and the fishes and the birds, and then he made animals. Here he is with some of them. Can you tell what they are? Some of them are rather difficult to recognise because I expect the artist had never seen the animal in real life, but was just copying pictures he had seen. Still, it is easy to recognise the elephant. Below come the rabbit and the cat and the squirrel, the lion and the dog, the ram and the goat, and the ox and the horse and the deer. These artists must have been very fond of animals, they draw so beautifully the ones they know. I like the ones on Pl. XXI particularly, they are so full of life. I think that artist must have seen a lion, but not, do you think, the monk who did the picture of Daniel in the lion's den (Pl. XXVI)? I like the way the artists often draw animals as if the animals were in the secret, and understood what was happening; look at the asses in Pls. XXXIII and XXXVI and XXXVIII. These books of beasts, Bestiaries they are called, are all about animals, with a picture and a story about each one. The stories are mostly very old, though the picture books did not become popular in England till about this date, the end of the twelfth century. But now we must go back to the story of the creation.

from the Book of Beasts at Oxford

VI

Last of all God made man and woman. In this picture Adam is already
created. God is making Eve. On the right is Adam asleep, God is
bending over him very carefully, he has taken the rib out of his side;
look, it is in his hand. On the other side are God and Eve (her name is
written beside her). She is just waking up for the first time and she looks up
to God who holds her hand. One can see that she loves him straight away.
In the middle of the picture is a ladder leading straight to heaven. The
door is open wide, there is St Michael standing by it and many other angels.
The ladder reminds one of Jacob's ladder (look at Pl. XIII). But Adam and
Eve did not need to be asleep to see it because the door was not closed then.
The Garden of Eden was very near to heaven. The Bible tells us that God
used to walk there in the cool of the day; it looks as if the angels often went in
and out too. What a lovely place it must have been!

Do you see that some of the angels inside the gate are carrying things? One
has the key to the gate, the next one a book, the one after a musical instrument
and the one on the right a palm branch. I wonder if the artist has given the
angel the palm branch because he knows that one day a son of Adam will
win a great victory. Our Lord is sometimes called the second Adam. Through
Adam we were all turned out of Paradise, through Jesus we are all rescued
and offered a new life even more wonderful than Paradise. I expect that the
book that the angel is carrying is the same that our Lord is carrying in the very
first picture (Frontispiece), the books which St John saw in heaven, one with
the names of everyone who shall be saved and others with the good and bad
deeds of everyone who ever lived. Now the book is quite blank because it is
the very beginning. The first mark is the terrible blot which Adam and Eve
made when they ate the apple which God had forbidden to them.

You remember how Satan tempted them. He was very angry and jealous
in Hell when he saw how happy Adam and Eve were. '*We must think eagerly
how to avenge ourselves on Adam, if we may turn heaven from the race of men. Let us
contrive that they may lose God's favour and turn away from his command. Then,
angry, He will cast them into hell, in these grim depths, and we shall have them for our
servants, the sons of men! If any of you can contrive that they should forsake God's
word and teaching, for him who achieves this, the reward is ready. Let him pass out
through the darkness and fly along the clouds to where Adam and Eve stand, wound
about with happiness.*' One of the devils was ready; *he began to prepare himself,
ready in his armour. He had a faithless heart. He knew many speeches and wicked
words. He wound his way up through Hell doors.* The Anglo-Saxon poetry book
has many fascinating pictures of how the devil tempted Eve, how in the end

He made Adam and Eve in Paradise

from the Anglo-Saxon Poetry Book

they ate the apple, and how God found them, hiding in the garden, but I have not room for them all.

VII

This picture is from another book about 150 years later. Here Adam and Eve are being turned out of the Garden of Eden. God is standing beside the Tree of Life, the scroll he holds in his hand says that they must be turned out lest they should eat the fruit of that tree too, and live for ever. St John saw the tree again in heaven, perhaps we shall be allowed to eat of it when we get there. Between Adam and Eve and the tree stands an angel with a flaming sword. Right in the corner is the gateway that they must go through.

Below they are already outside; the angel is giving Adam a spade so that he may dig and grow his own food, and Eve a distaff which will spin sheep's wool into thread so that she can weave clothes for them both. God had said that now they must work, now it will be hard for them to grow enough to eat and they will get hurt and in the end they will die. We are all the children of Adam so we have to die like him, but it is a good thing that we are all bound up together because then we are bound up with the Second Adam too. Adam and Eve look very unhappy and sorry for their disobedience so in the end God forgave them. You can see him in Pl. XLII. The first thing he did after his victory was to rescue them out of Hell and take them with him to heaven.

The bottom picture shows what happened after man had started to disobey God. There are Cain and Abel. Cain is a farmer and Abel a shepherd. They have brought some of the fruits of their work to offer to God, as I expect Adam taught them. Abel has brought a lamb and Cain a sheaf of corn. God was pleased with Abel's offering and not with Cain's; I expect he offered it grudgingly and did not really want to please God. Cain was jealous and when he and Abel were alone in a field together he took the bone of an animal and killed Abel. But God saw what he did.

They were turned out of Paradise

from the Psalter of Bishop Henry of Blois

VIII

After Cain other men did wrong, they learned how to do clever things, how to build cities, how to make music, how to work metal, they wanted to make themselves as grand as the angels, instead of wanting to please God and serve him. God was very angry. You remember something terrible happened, he sent the Flood and everyone was drowned except Noah and his family. Noah was not a descendant of Cain, but of Seth, Adam's third son; he was a just man, who walked with God, remembering him all the time, thinking all the day how he could please him. Here is Noah in the ark which God told him to build. 'Make thee an ark of timber planks, rooms shalt thou make in the ark, and shalt pitch it within and without with pitch, a window shalt thou make to the ark and the door of the ark shalt thou set in the side thereof; with lower, second and third stories shalt thou make it.' The artist has drawn it just as the Bible says, only he has made it much taller than it should be, to make it fit better into the page. His ship is an Anglo-Saxon one with a great dragon-headed prow. But look at the angels who guard it, and there is God himself holding open the door, ready to shut them all in safely. The animals are all in, there is Noah holding the steering oar; only his wife seems reluctant to go on board. I expect she does not like leaving her home and all the things she has been used to, to go into this queer boat when it seems quite unnecessary, for the Flood has not come yet. But that is what we all have to do, because the history of the Flood is more than a story about Noah, it was a foreshadowing of what God was going to do for men. The ark that he told Noah to make and that he looked after so carefully is a picture of his Church, and the Flood is like life. There may be great storms, we may seem alone and adrift but we are safe in the ark and it will bring us to heaven in the end. But we have to be ready to leave the dry land and commit ourselves to the sea and to leave behind whatever God thinks is unnecessary.

On the top storey Noah is sending out the raven and at the next window is the dove with an olive branch. The raven flew away and never came back. Those are the people who seem to be in the Church but do not really belong there, whose hearts are black because they do not love God. The dove reminds us of the Holy Ghost, whom God sent on Whitsunday to be with his Church. There he is on Pl. XLV filling the hearts and minds of the apostles. The dove brought Noah an olive branch, that was a sign of the peace that is in the church, and also of the grace which God has poured, like olive oil, on all her members. You remember how on Palm Sunday (Pl. XXXVIII) the people came to meet our Lord with branches of olive. The

God told Noah how to build the Ark

from the Anglo-Saxon Poetry Book

prayers on Palm Sunday tell us that this was to signify the same things as the olive branch brought by the dove so long before.

IX

This is the tower of Babel built by Nimrod the mighty hunter, and his cousins. They were the grandsons and great-grandsons of Noah, but like the descendants of Cain they were very proud of their own cleverness, and forgot that it was God who had given it to them. They thought that they would make a tower which would reach to heaven. It is a very fine tower. It is made of blue and red and yellow bricks and the roof of rounded tiles. I expect the artist has made it like an Anglo-Saxon palace and it shows us how they built their houses. On the left is a scaffolding and the workmen seem to be handing up great stone slabs. The man on the first floor is pinning tiles on to the front of the house with nails, and below they are fastening the great hinges of the door. This picture is from another Anglo-Saxon translation of the Bible. It was made by Aelfric the Grammarian, who was a pupil of St Aethelwold (see Pl. XXXVIII) at Winchester and later Abbot of the monasteries at Cerne and Eynsham. He is famous for his writings and his learning. But look, God has come to see what the people are doing. He is there on the left at the top of the ladder with his angel beside him. He is not pleased with the people. He had not created them to set their hearts on building grand cities and towers on earth. He wanted them instead to set their hearts on the city he had prepared for them in heaven. So he said to his angel, 'Go to, let us go down and there confound their language that they may not understand one another's speech.' So the Lord 'scattered them abroad from thence upon the face of all the earth, and they left off to build the city. Therefore is the name of it called Babel, because the Lord did there confound the language of all the earth'. God showed them that it was not the right way to get to heaven, not even the right way to build a house, 'Except the Lord build the house they labour in vain that build it.' It is no good our making great plans if God does not approve of them, we should first ask him to bless them. Jacob's ladder (Pl. XIII) was the way which really led from earth to heaven.

Men tried to build the Tower of Babel by themselves

from Aelfric's Anglo-Saxon translation of Genesis

X

But God was not going to let men go on doing stupid things. He was going to show them the right way. The man he chose to show it was Abraham.

The top picture shows Abraham (he is the tall one in front) and his servants and his flocks. The Bible said he had sheep and oxen and he-asses and menservants and maidservants and she-asses and camels. They look as if they were setting out on a journey. Abraham made many journeys. God called to him to leave his country and his family, the cities in which he had been brought up, Ur of the Chaldees, and Haran, because he said that he wanted to give him a land and make him the father of a great nation 'and in thy seed shall all the nations of the earth be blessed'. What God meant was that our Lord was going to be Abraham's descendant and that he was going to be the father of all Christian people. When he saved Noah in the ark God promised that he would never again destroy mankind, and now to Abraham he has promised that one day it shall be blessed again. But first Abraham, like Noah, had to leave everything to follow God's command, and had to believe his promise even when it seemed almost impossible; for he was only a stranger and a wanderer in the land of Canaan, which God had said was to be his, and he and his wife were growing old and still they had no son. But God gave him many signs to show that he was with him. The lower picture shows us one. Abraham has just won a battle against four kings who had taken his nephew Lot captive. As he came home a stranger came to meet him, 'Melchizedek, King of Salem, the priest of the most high God,' bringing bread and wine. He blessed Abraham, and Abraham gave him a tenth of all the spoil that he had won. There is Abraham on the steps of the altar offering him a sheep. St Paul explains who Melchisedek was. He was not like the other kings in the story. They belonged to the various cities of Canaan. His name means king of justice, and Salem means peace, so he was king of justice and peace. 'That is all; no name of father or mother, no pedigree, no date of birth or of death; there he stands eternally a priest, the true figure of the Son of God.' You see he is dressed like a priest, and he carries the things, the bread and wine, that our Lord was going to use in his own sacrifice so long after. That is why our Lord is called 'a priest after the order of Melchisedek'. To-day when we offer our Lord's own sacrifice we remember these old sacrifices which foreshadowed it, and we ask God to accept it as he accepted 'the gifts of his just servant Abel and the sacrifice of our patriarch Abraham and that which thy high priest Melchisedek offered to thee'. Abraham seems to know that he is meeting someone much greater than himself; look how

Abraham the great traveller

from Aelfric's Anglo-Saxon translation of Genesis

Melchisedek comes to meet him

from a manuscript of a poem by Prudentius

humble he is and Melchisedek looks very gentle and welcoming and young, like our Lord.

XI

The next sign that God gave Abraham was easier for him to understand. One day he was sitting in the door of his tent, in the heat of the day, and he looked up and saw three men standing by him. He invited them to rest under the tree and hastened to tell his wife Sarah to get a meal ready for them. When it was ready he stood by while they ate. Look how politely and graciously he is greeting them and waiting on them. They said to him, 'Where is Sarah thy wife?' and he said, 'Behold in the tent.' You can see her right at the side of the picture, listening to what they are saying. 'Sarah thy wife shall have a son.' She laughed, she thought that she and Abraham were too old to have children, and she had been barren all her life. Abraham knew now that it was God who was appearing to him in the shape of the three men. (Perhaps God came as three men to give us an idea of the Trinity? He had not told any one about the Trinity yet.) The Lord said to Abraham, 'Wherefore did Sarah laugh? Is anything too hard for the Lord? At the time appointed I will return unto thee and Sarah shall have a son.' So Sarah was given her son Isaac. When he was born she said, 'God hath made me to laugh so that all that hear will laugh with me.' Let us all be glad too because this is the son of God's promise. He had made it clear that this birth was his work, a special gift, a miracle, not something which was coming to men through their own work, or naturally, by right, but something God was giving out of his love. That is why the promise to Abraham's heirs had to be through this son, Isaac, and not through his elder son Ishmael, a child of Sarah's slave, Hagar. Ishmael and Hagar had to be rejected, as the picture on the next page shows.

God gave yet another sign of what was to come, through Abraham. When Isaac was a little boy God told his father to take him to the top of a mountain and there to make a sacrifice of him. What faith and obedience Abraham had! He did not argue with God, but took the son of whom so many promises had been made, and made ready to kill him. Here they are at the top of the mountain. Isaac is on the altar, Abraham has drawn his sword. But the angel has caught it. Look, there is God's hand in the sky and the angel is pointing to the ram which is caught in the thicket, which is to be sacrificed instead. But when it was the only Son of God who was on the

The Angels promise him a Son

from the Lambeth Bible

But God asks him to sacrifice Isaac

from the Psalter at Glasgow

altar of the cross, God allowed him to be really sacrificed. So much more he gives us than he has ever asked of any one! You remember Abraham made Isaac carry the wood for the burnt offering up the hill. That was for an extra sign that Isaac was, as it were, acting the part of Christ, to help people to understand what was going to happen. For did not our Lord have to carry the wood of his cross up the hill to Calvary?

XII

Here is Isaac when he was an old man. He holds his hands up to his face and his eyes are blind. He knows he will die soon. He is telling Esau his eldest son to go and kill some venison and prepare a dish of it for him; that was the custom, so that he might give him his blessing. There is Esau on the left with his bow and his dog, looking for deer. Beside Isaac is his wife Rebecca. Now Rebecca knew that the blessing was really meant for Jacob, their younger son, because before the children were born God had told her that she would have twin sons, and that the elder should serve the younger. So while Esau was hunting she made Jacob put on his brother's clothes, and she put goat skins on his hands to make them seem like Esau's hands, which were very hairy (you can see that in the picture) and she gave him savoury meat and sent him to his father. And Isaac gave him the blessing. Isaac knew that the blessing he was giving was a very special one, 'God give thee of the dew of heaven, let people serve thee and nations bow down to thee;' it was God's blessing, not his own, and when he found that he had given it to Jacob instead of Esau he was frightened, not angry, and trembled very exceedingly. But Esau had never really valued his right as the eldest son. Long before when he was very hungry he had said to Jacob that he would sell him his birthright for a mess of pottage. He had thought that having enough to eat to-day was more important than God's promise of heaven. That was not like Abraham's faith! Nor like what our Lord was going to teach.

You remember the same thing had happened before to Ishmael, Abraham's eldest son; he too had been rejected in favour of his brother Isaac. In the lower picture Abraham is sending him and his mother away into the wilderness. He has given Hagar some bread and a bottle of water for the journey, and she has put them in her basket. It was Sarah who made Abraham send them away. He was very loth, but God told him that it was right and that he would look after them. Again God was making people act in their lives the meaning of what was going to happen in history. Ishmael was

The elder sons are rejected; Esau loses his blessing

Ishmael is sent into the Wilderness

from Aelfric's Anglo-Saxon translation of Genesis

Abraham's son but he was the son of a slave. He was like the covenant God made with the Israelites, when he gave the law to Moses (see Pl. XIV). They were his chosen people, but they had to obey, to serve God according to the law, with fear. But Isaac is the son of the free woman, Sarah; he is like God's New Covenant, Our Lord's Covenant, when he came to make us sons of God, instead of slaves, to live according to the spirit, in freedom. That is why Esau and Ishmael had to be rejected to show us that the New Testament was one day going to replace the Old.

XIII

This is Jacob's dream. He had been sent by his father from Canaan to Mesopotamia to find himself a wife belonging to the family of Abraham. He was going to find his wife Rachel. One evening on his journey when the sun set he took some stones to make himself a pillow (they seem very big ones) and lay down and slept. 'And he dreamed, and behold a ladder set up on the earth, and the top of it reached to heaven; and behold the angels of God ascending and descending on it and behold the Lord stood above it.' There is God at the very top of the ladder speaking to Jacob, and making the same promise to him that he made to Abraham. 'The land whereon thou liest, to thee will I give it, and to thy seed; and thy seed shall be as the dust of the earth, and thou shalt spread abroad to the West, and to the East, and to the North, and to the South; and in thee and in thy seed shall all the families of the earth be blessed.' How near God came to Jacob! He was afraid and said, 'How dreadful is this place! this is none other than the house of God, and this the gate of Heaven.'

For the ladder he sees is really Our Lord. It is he who is the Gate into heaven for us, who was going to open the door and let down the ladder so that men on earth should no longer be separated from heaven, as they had been since Adam's sin had cut us off from that first ladder that we saw in the Garden of Eden (Pl. VI). And the angels go up and down the ladder because it is not just a ladder that we can climb when we die, but ever since he became a ladder, a man as well as God, one foot in heaven and one on earth, Our Lord has been with us. The angels keep coming down to help us and prophets and saints have been able to go up and look into heaven and tell us about it, like Isaiah and St John the Evangelist.

I expect the monk who drew this picture was thinking too of what St Benedict said about Jacob's ladder in his Rule, which was probably read in

Cingulaſ iacob. 7phaım de lege. 7 templo. 7palſione xp̄ı. que int̄ra illa figura eranr. Terribił cū̄. lex.
dom̄ ſi. templii. palſio vp̄ı. apuo pont̄e celi.

from Aelfric's Anglo-Saxon translation of Genesis

his monastery every day. St Benedict says that we must make our lives like a ladder going up to God, and the angels descending and ascending show us how. We go up when we are humble and think nothing of ourselves, but directly we begin to think grandly of ourselves, we go down. Because we have to learn that it is only through God's help that we can climb the ladder at all.

That is a rather different idea of the ladder from the first one. All these stories have so many meanings, different ways of teaching us about God and life. I should like to tell you many more! But it is important not to get them muddled, but to think about each one separately.

XIV

A lot has happened between this picture and the last. The first picture here shows Moses on Mount Sinai. God's first promise to Abraham is soon going to be fulfilled, that he should be the father of a great nation, and should have the land of Canaan. You remember how Joseph, Jacob's son, went into Egypt, and then how his other brothers came because of the famine, and they all settled there. There they multiplied exceedingly and became a people and then God told Moses to lead them out of Egypt. He did great signs for them before Pharoah and the Egyptians to show that they were God's chosen people, and then he led them through the Red Sea into the desert. Before they came to the Promised Land they had to be given a law and they had to be purified in the desert. They had to leave their ordinary way of living and live alone with God, just as so many saints went into the desert to learn to know God, or into a desert of living without any of the things they liked, and as our Lord went into the desert to fast and pray before he started his work of teaching. Now they are in the desert and God has called Moses up to the top of Mount Sinai. Down below all the people are waiting. They had made themselves ready as they were told, and washed their clothes and in the morning as they stood there 'there were thunders and lightnings, and a thick cloud upon the Mount and the voice of the trumpet exceeding loud, and Mount Sinai was altogether on a smoke, because the Lord descended upon it in fire, and the smoke ascended as the smoke of a furnace and the whole Mount quaked greatly. And when the voice of the trumpet sounded long and waxed louder and louder the Lord called Moses up to the top of the Mount, and Moses went up'. God spoke to Moses; he gave him the ten commandments and many other laws. There is the hand of God holding a

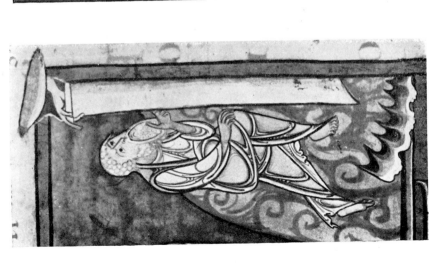

God gives the law to Moses

And be teaches tbe people

from the Lambeth Bible

from the Bury St Edmunds Bible

great scroll, showing the laws to Moses. After that God called him up a second time to the mountain; this time he stayed there forty days and forty nights and God told him how he was to make a tabernacle and an ark, of the sort of sacrifices which he wanted, and how Aaron and his sons were to be priests. At the end Moses asked something for himself. He said to God, 'I beseech thee show me thy glory.' God said, 'Thou canst not see my face and live,' but he showed him a little of his glory and it was so wonderful that when Moses came down from the mountain his face shone so that the people were afraid to come near him.

In the second picture he is teaching them all the law as God had taught it to him. Behind him is God, still very near, and inspiring all his words. The people look very thoughtful and attentive. You can see the light shining from his face in two great horns.

XV

Here are the Levites carrying the Ark which the Israelites have made just as Moses told them. They are still wandering in the desert, so wherever they moved they had to take down the Tabernacle which was like a tent and pack up and carry with them the Ark and all the holy things. Only the Levites were allowed to do it. There is Aaron, the chief priest, Moses' brother, in the middle. In front of him is the Ark and the Veil which was hung before it. That is the veil which 'was torn this way and that, from top to bottom' when our Lord died, for then there was no more use for the Ark and the Tabernacle. Behind Aaron are other Levites; they are carrying the curtains of the Tabernacle, and its pillars and their sockets and pins and cords; others are carrying vessels. Now that they had made the Ark and the Tabernacle the Israelites had a sign that God was with them all the time, 'for the cloud of the Lord was upon the Tabernacle by day and fire was on it by night in the sight of all the house of Israel, throughout all their journeys.' Moses did not need to go up to the mountain now, he met God in the tabernacle. God taught them too how they must make sacrifices to him there, not that he had any need of anything that they could give him, but to prepare them for the sacrifice which was to come when our Lord poured out his own blood to wash us clean.

All this time they were in the desert, forty years separated from other people. God fed them on manna which came down from heaven. That was another sign of the sacrifice to come, the food we have from heaven now, his Body in Holy Communion.

[40]

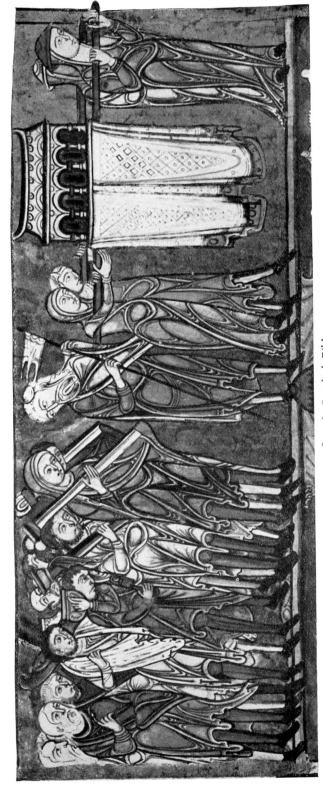

The Israelites carry the Ark through the Wilderness

from the Lambeth Bible

I expect you have noticed that the last pictures are different from those of the Anglo-Saxon poetry book. They are much later, after the Norman conquest. They are pictures from the great Bibles that monks started to make in the twelfth century, books so big and heavy that one can hardly carry them. There are the Winchester Bible, the Bury St Edmunds Bible, the Dover Bible, the Lambeth Bible and some others. They were made by the monks for their own or other monasteries and were used to read from during meals, but they were so beautiful that they became famous, and I expect many people asked to look at them. The first letter of each book in the Bible is usually drawn very large and a picture of some story in the book drawn inside (like Pls. XIX, XX, XXIII and XXVI). Some of the Bibles also have full page pictures at the beginning of each book, telling a story in several scenes (like Pl. XXV). In some of our plates I have taken just a part of one these big pages (Pls. XIA, XIV, XV, XVIIIA, XXVII).

XVI

And now at last they have come to the Promised Land. But it was not Moses who brought them there, for holy as he was he represented the Law, which was going to be superseded (Pl. XII). The Promised Land of Canaan for the Jews was a sign of the Promised Land of Heaven for all men, so the leader who took them in was Joshua, for Joshua is the same name as Jesus.

This picture is an illustration to the psalm, 'Laudate Nomen Domini,' which praises God for all his goodness to Israel, remembering all the wonderful things he has done. It was written in Jerusalem, long after they first arrived. There is Jerusalem, the walled city in the middle. They have set up the Tabernacle on the rock on the hill, and in it an altar. Beside are the Levites carrying lutes. It is they who are singing the psalm to God, who is at the top in the middle. Outside the walls are the people going out to measure the land and divide it between the tribes. They are taking measuring rods and chains. In the background we can see all the things that happened on their journey from Egypt. On the right I think is what happened before they left Egypt. There are the angels in heaven raining down, all the plagues upon the Egyptians. There are their first-born, both men and oxen, lying dead upon the ground, and there in the water is a man and his horse, one of Pharoah's army which was drowned in the Red Sea. How astonished those people in the boat must have been when they saw the waters of the sea divide, let the Israelites pass, and then roll back and overwhelm all the army of the Egyptians.

They come into the Promised Land

from the Canterbury Psalm Picture Book

The people on the left must be those who the Israelites found when they left the desert and came down into the land of Canaan, when God gave them the victory over all the kings who lived there so that they could take possession of their land. There on horses are Sihon, King of the Amorites, Og, King of Bashan, and one of the other kings. God sent great hailstones against them. You can see a great storm coming down from heaven.

At the sides at the top you can see two fenced cities, and on pedestals the idols worshipped by the people of the cities; one on the left has fallen already, and those on the right are being knocked down by the moon! That is the sun on the left and the moon on the right, in circles. I expect the moon is taking part because Joshua asked God to make the sun and the moon stand still on the day of their battle against the Amorites. 'And the sun stood still and the moon stayed until the people had avenged themselves upon their enemies. For the Lord fought for Israel.' No wonder that the idols fell, for they were only the works of men's hands, 'they have a mouth but they speak not; eyes have they but they do not see; ears have they but they hear not: neither is there any breath in their mouths.' No wonder that they fell before the people of the living God!

XVII

This is the story of Ruth. She lived in the time of the judges when the Israelites were first settled in Palestine. In the top picture she is gleaning corn—picking up the stray stalks which the reapers have dropped in making up their sheaves. She is in the field of Boaz. Ruth was a Moabitess who had married an Israelite who had come with his father and his family to live in Moab because of a famine. Now he and his father and brother are dead, and Ruth has been left with her mother-in-law Naomi. Naomi wanted to go back to her own country so she said to her daughters-in-law, 'Go, return each to her mother's house. The Lord deal kindly with you as ye have dealt with the dead and with me.' One of them went back to her home, but Ruth said, 'Whither thou goest I will go, and where thou lodgest I will lodge, thy people shall be my people and thy God my God.' So they went back to Naomi's city which was Bethlehem. And so Ruth went out into the field of Naomi's kinsman, Boaz, to see if she might be allowed to glean corn for food for them both. Boaz saw her. He is the tall figure with a great scroll, perhaps he is counting up his fields and his harvest. He was kind to her and gave her dinner with his workpeople and told his men, 'Let fall some of the handfuls

[44]

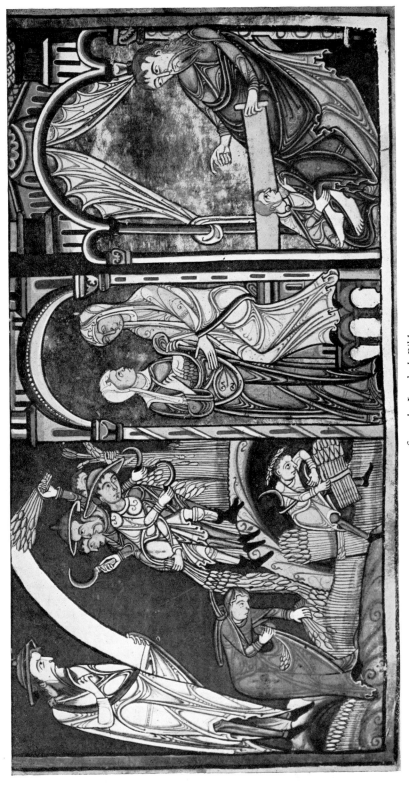

The Story of Ruth

from the Lambeth Bible

of purpose for her, and leave them that she may glean them and rebuke her not.' So in the evening she brought home all the barley she had gleaned and some of the food from her dinner which she had kept back, and gave it to Naomi. There they are together, very happy in the kindness of Boaz and their love of one another. When the harvest was over Naomi told Ruth to go to the threshing floor and after the feast, when Boaz was asleep, she was to uncover his feet and lie down by his feet. There she is doing as she was told. So Boaz took Ruth and she became his wife and she had a son and she called him Obed. All her friends said to Naomi, 'Blessed be the Lord which hath not left thee this day without a kinsman that his name may be famous in Israel, and he shall be unto thee a restorer of thy life and a nourisher of thine old age, for thy daughter-in-law which loveth thee, which is better to thee than seven sons, hath borne him.' Obed was the father of Jesse, who was the father of David.

It is Ruth of whom Isaiah said, 'Send thou a lamb, O Lord, as ruler of the land from the rock of the wilderness (that is Moab) to the mount of the daughter of Zion.' Her descendant through David was going to be Ruler. I think she is like a lamb, she was so obedient and humble and loving.

XVIII

These are pictures of Hannah, the mother of Samuel, and of Saul. The Bible tells us that Hannah was very unhappy because she had no child. 'And she was in bitterness of soul, and prayed unto the Lord and wept sore. And she vowed a vow, 'If thou wilt give unto thine handmaid a man child, then, I will give him unto the Lord all the days of his life.' God gave her a son, Samuel, and she gave him back to God, to be his priest. Here she is making her prayer of thanksgiving. 'My heart rejoiceth in the Lord, mine horn is exalted in the Lord: my mouth is enlarged over mine enemies, because I rejoice in thy salvation. There is none holy as the Lord, for there is none beside thee, neither is there any rock like our God.' What a beautiful prayer! Surely it is more than the prayer of an ordinary mother over her baby? It is also a prayer of the Holy Ghost who is making Hannah speak as if she were the Church, the mother of us all. That is why she goes on to say, 'The Lord killeth and maketh alive, he bringeth down to hell and bringeth back again. He raiseth up the poor out of the dust.' She is prophesying about our Lord who became poor and died for us and rose again.

I think the artist has made Hannah look very like the Church, with her

Hannah who hoped in God

from the Bury St Edmunds Bible

Saul who disobeyed God

from the Lambeth Bible

heart and mind all turned to God, putting all her trust in him and singing his song for ever and ever.

The other picture is a very sad one. It is the death of Saul. You remember Samuel anointed him to be king, because the Israelites wanted a king, but he did not do what God told him to do. So God took his Spirit away from him, and he became very unhappy, and jealous of David, whom he persecuted. In the end he died in a battle against the Philistines. His disobedience has led to just the same things as that of Adam, to unhappiness and hatred and killing.

They are like the two cities of which St Augustine tells us, these two figures. The city of those who love God, all the true members of the Church, who look upwards and seek to do God's will, and have peace in their hearts; and the earthly city of those who think about power and riches and comfort, who look downwards to the things of this world and find in the end nothing but loneliness and fighting and death.

XIX

This is the story of David and Goliath. It happened before Saul was dead, while he was still king. The Philistines had a champion called Goliath, his height was nine and a half feet and the staff of his spear was like a weaver's beam, he was so strong. None of the Israelites dared to fight with him. David was only a shepherd boy; he was not old enough to be in Saul's army like his brothers, but he came to the camp to bring them some food from his father, Jesse, the grandson of Ruth. He saw Goliath come, as he had come every day to defy the Israelites to fight him, and David said, 'Who is this uncircumcised Philistine that he should defy the armies of the living God?' And he said to Saul, 'Let no man's heart fail him, thy servant will go and fight with this Philistine.' There he is, a little boy, going up to Goliath, swinging his sling (it is difficult to make out the sling because the picture is rather rubbed). Goliath disdained him. 'Am I a dog that thou comest at me with staves?' But David answered, 'Thou comest at me with a sword and with a spear and with a shield: but I come to thee in the name of the Lord of Hosts.' Which is stronger? Look, Goliath has fallen; there is David cutting off his head with his own sword.

St Augustine tells us that that teaches how we too can win a victory against any temptation no matter how big it seems. 'See the little David against the great, but placing reliance on the name of the Lord. Thou camest to me, he said, with a shield and a spear, I in the name of Almighty God.

David fights Goliath

And kills him

from the Dover Bible

Thus, thus, in no other way, in no other way whatever, is the enemy laid prostrate.' Somewhere else St Augustine says that David's stone killed Goliath because it hit him on the forehead, because he had never been marked with the cross there. (Look at Pl. XXVII; everyone's forehead must be marked with the cross.) That is what makes us strong, the cross which makes and keeps us Christians.

XX

Here on the next picture is David singing and making poetry. At the top he is the king he became after Saul's death; he is playing a psaltery and the bells he is striking at the same time are gold. There is a lady with him playing a pipe. I wonder who she is? Below, he is still the shepherd that he was when he fought Goliath. He is sitting solitary on the hills with only the animals to listen. I expect it is near Bethlehem where he was born. He looks very like a poet, like Orpheus singing about the beauty of the world, or like the saints who went to live in the desert who made friends with animals, or like our Lord. I expect he talked to the animals when he was in the wilderness.

A shepherd and a king, born at Bethlehem. Who does that remind you of? Who was the good Shepherd? Like Melchisedek, David is a figure of Christ who was going to be his descendant. In so many ways he was like him. David was anointed, and that is what 'Christ' means; he was like a priest too; you remember he ate the holy bread which was kept on the altar in the Tabernacle. He was persecuted by Saul as our Lord was persecuted by the Jews; and all the time he loved his enemies. He would not hurt Saul though in the cave of Engedi he was in his power. How much love there is in the lament he made over the death of Saul and Jonathan, and over that of his own rebellious son Absolom! How angry he was with the people who expected to please him by killing his enemies! And above all how he loved God. He was not ashamed, when they brought the Ark into Jerusalem at last, to take off his grand clothes and show his joy by dancing before the Lord with all his might, because he was humble and loving like a child.

And so we can understand what was shadowed by the fight of David and Goliath. It was our Lord in the weakness and littleness of his nature as a man, fighting against the Devil and all the power of sin and wickedness. It was the great fight he came to earth to make. He was our champion. And so after the fight David reigned in the earthly Jerusalem, as a shadow of our Lord's reign in the New Jerusalem, which we hope to see when we die.

from the Dover Bible

But David foreshadowed our Lord even in his poetry, the Psalms. They are full of words which seem to be said by our Lord himself, about his own life, and when he came he said that He had meant that to be so. That is why the Church uses the Psalms every day in her prayers. Perhaps the lady in the picture helping David to play is the Church herself helping him to make songs for her.

XXI

This is a picture of one of the songs which he sang, Psalm 103 (104), 'Benedic anima mea Domino.' I think it must have been one of the songs he sang in the hills; it is about how God upholds, all the time looks after, keeps order, in all his creation.

'O Lord my God, what magnificence is thine! Glory and beauty are thy clothing. The light is a garment thou dost wrap around thee, the heavens a curtain thy hand unfolds. On the wings of the wind thou dost come and go. Thou wilt have thy angels be like the winds, the servants that wait on thee like a flame of fire.' There is God in heaven standing on the winds, his angels round him. 'The earth thou hast planted on its own firm base, undisturbed for all time. He sends the torrents down the ravines, water-courses among the hills that may give drink to every beast of the field; here the wild asses may slake their thirst.' There on the left are the asses braying, and sitting quietly by the stream are sheep and oxen. 'Thy hand gives earth all her plenty. Grass must grow for the cattle; for men too she must put forth her shoots, if thou art to bring corn out of the earth; if there is to be wine that will rejoice man's heart, oil to make his face shine, and bread that will keep man's strength from failing.' There are the men sitting at the table in the centre. One servant is bringing them wine, another is pouring oil over a man's head. On the left are the great trees, 'cedars of Lebanon, trees of the Lord's own planting. Here it is the birds build their nests; the stork makes its home in the fir branches.' On the other side are the high hills where the harts take refuge, and the stony places where the hedgehogs have their caves. 'He has given us the moon for our calendar, the sun knows well the hour of his setting' (do you see them in the sky, on either side?), 'in the night all the forest is astir with prowling beasts; the young lions go roaring after their prey, God's pensioners, asking for their food. Then the sun rises, and they meet to lie down in their dens, while man goes abroad to toil till evening.' There he is with his plough and his oxen. The man on the right above the lions is David, singing his song, praising God for all these things. And there at the bottom lies the vast

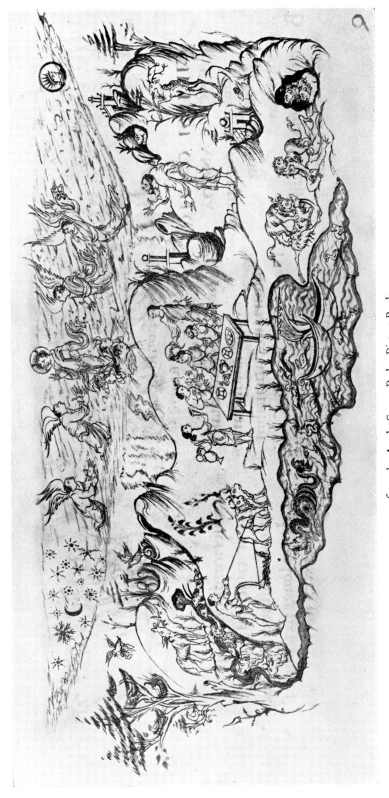

This is his song when he was happy

from the Anglo-Saxon Psalm Picture Book

ocean, peopled with living things past number, great creatures and small. There go the ships, and that is that Leviathan. 'And all look to thee to send them their food at the appointed time, thy hand opens and all are filled with content. But see thou hidest thy face and they breathe no more, they go back to the dust which they came from. Send forth thy spirit and we shall be re-created, and the face of the earth shall be renewed!'

XXII

That was a song of happiness, of God's providence maintaining order throughout creation. This is an illustration of someone in great distress Psalm 30 (31). In te Domine speravi.

David is holding out his hands to the angel of God, who is saving him from the devil who is trying to catch him. You can see how he is in trouble; he is alone, with no friends to help him. 'I am forgotten, as one dead, out of mind: I am become like a broken vessel.' There is the pot beside him, falling down, all the water spilt. There seems to be no ground under his feet; it is as if he were falling down a precipice, and below are his enemies waiting to catch him. 'While they assembled against me, they plotted to take away my life.' But he turns to God to help him, 'But in thee O Lord, do I put my trust; I said thou art my God, my lot is in thy hands. Deliver me out of the hands of mine enemies! Into thy hands I commend my spirit: thou hast re-deemed me O Lord God of truth.' Look how eagerly the angel stretches out his hands to help him. He will hold him and he will be safe.

Do you remember those words, 'Into thy hands I commend my spirit?' They are our Lord's last words on the Cross. In another psalm there are those other words that he said, 'My God, my God, why hast thou forsaken me.' The Psalms tell us not only what David himself knew of unhappiness, but what our Lord knew too. They make up, in a sense, what is left out in the gospel story of our Lord's Passion. There it only tells us what happened; here it gives us a suggestion of what he felt, how being a man he felt all the fear and misery that we can feel. That is why in Holy Week the Church sings these Psalms in the evening after she has read us the story of the Passion in the morning.

His song in the time of trouble

from the Anglo-Saxon Psalm Picture Book

XXIII

After the death of David and Solomon, his son, the Israelites started to forget all the wonderful things God had done for them. God sent them great prophets to remind them. Here are two, Elijah and Elisha. Elijah's work is done and God has come to fetch him. He and Elisha were talking together, 'and it came to pass as they still went on and talked, that, behold, there appeared a chariot of fire and horses of fire, and parted them both asunder, and Elijah went up by a whirlwind into heaven. And Elisha saw it, and he cried, "My father, my father, the chariot of Israel, and the horsemen thereof."' Those are the words written on the scroll. 'And he saw him no more. And he took hold of his own clothes, and rent them in two pieces. He took up also the mantle of Elijah that fell from him, and went back, and stood by the bank of Jordan.' Look how firmly God holds Elijah by the hand and how gladly he goes to him. There is his cloak falling down to Elisha below who is ready to do the work now. You remember Elijah had first called him to follow him and be a prophet by throwing his cloak over him when he was ploughing in the field, and now with the same cloak he did his first miracle, 'he took the mantle of Elijah that fell from him, and smote the waters, and said, "Where is the Lord God of Elijah?" and when he also had smitten the waters they parted hither and thither, and Elisha went over.' He did many other great miracles, as Elijah had done. But still the kings of Israel kept forgetting about God, and worshipping other gods, those gods who have eyes and see not, and ears that hear not. They seemed quite to have forgotten the promise to Abraham that was still to come.

from the Dover Bible

XXIV

God sent another prophet to tell them more about that promise, Isaiah. This is a picture of his prophecy. He said, 'And there shall come forth a rod out of the root of Jesse, a flower shall rise up out of his root.' There at the bottom of the picture is Jesse and out of him rises a great tree, which turns into a lady, and out of the lady comes a flower surrounded by seven doves. The rod is our Lady, the flower is our Lord, the doves are the seven gifts of the Holy Ghost. Isaiah prophesied that they should rest upon him: 'the spirit of wisdom and of understanding, the spirit of counsel and of fortitude, the spirit of knowledge and of godliness. And he shall be filled with the spirit of the fear of the Lord. He shall judge the poor with justice, and shall reprove with equity for the meek of the earth. And justice shall be the girdle of his loins: and faith the girdle of his reins. The wolf shall dwell with the lamb: and the leopard shall lie down with the kid. The calf and the lion and the sheep shall abide together: and a little child shall lead them. They shall not hurt, nor shall they kill in all my holy mountain: for the earth shall be full of the knowledge of the Lord, as the waters cover the sea.'

In the two middle circles you can see the new and wonderful salvation which our Lord will bring. On the right Justice (with her scales) and Peace are kissing one another. On the left Mercy (with her pot of oil) and Truth are holding hands. Above, on either side, are two other ladies. One is crowned, she is the Church, the bride of Christ. She is led by two figures, probably St Peter and St Paul. On the right is the Synagogue. Moses is beside her (with horns) and the other may be Abraham. Look, God's hand is taking the veil away from her face because when Christ comes all the prophecies and foreshadowings of the Old Testament will become plain. All round are the prophets, in the bottom corners two kings, David and Solomon. I expect the ones in the bottom circles are Daniel, Isaiah (with scroll), Jeremiah and Ezekiel. Perhaps the ones at the very top are Micah, who prophesied that Christ would be born in Bethlehem, and Zechariah, who foretold how he should ride into Jerusalem on Palm Sunday.

from the Lambeth Bible

XXV

But the kings of Judah would not listen to Isaiah either, and in the end King Manasseh killed him. So God allowed their enemies to conquer first the kingdom of Israel and then that of Judah, and take their people into captivity. But even in captivity some were faithful to the living God. This is the story of Daniel and his three friends, at the court of Nebuchadnezzar, king of Babylon.

One night the king had a dream. He saw a great statue, its head was of gold, the breast and arms of silver, the belly and thighs of brass, the legs of iron and the feet part of iron and part of clay. (The silver in the picture has gone black and smudgy unfortunately.) Then he saw a stone 'cut out of a mountain without hands' which struck the statue upon its feet which were partly of clay, they broke in pieces, and the iron, the clay, the brass, the silver and the gold were all broken in pieces, and the pieces were carried away by the wind: and there was no place found for them. But the stone that struck the statue became a great mountain and filled the whole earth. Nebuchadnezzar was very frightened by his dream, but when he woke up he could not remember it. So he called all the wise men and magicians of his kingdom and said, 'The thing is gone from me; if ye will not make known unto me the dream, with the interpretation thereof, ye shall be cut in pieces.' There is the king on the right at the top, talking to them. They are saying that he has asked them to do something impossible. He was very angry and commanded that all the wise men in Babylon should be killed. Now Daniel and his friends were counted as wise men, and they came to kill them. In the picture below you see Daniel before the king asking if he might have a little time to see if he cannot explain the dream. There are Daniel's friends praying for him while he is asleep, and in his sleep God told him everything. There is the hand of God holding a scroll with all the interpretation of the dream. So Daniel went to the king and told him his dream, and how the statue represented the great kingdoms of the world, the golden head was Nebuchadnezzar's own kingdom, the silver and the brass and the iron were other kingdoms which would come after him. But the stone which grew into a great mountain is a kingdom which God will set up that shall consume all these kingdoms and it shall stand for ever. Nebuchadnezzar was amazed at the wisdom of Daniel and fell on his face and worshipped him and commanded that they should offer him incense. Look at the bottom picture on the left.

The stone is the Church which shall fill the whole earth. The statue is another idea of the earthly city, the Tower of Babel, which seems so grand but is not founded on God.

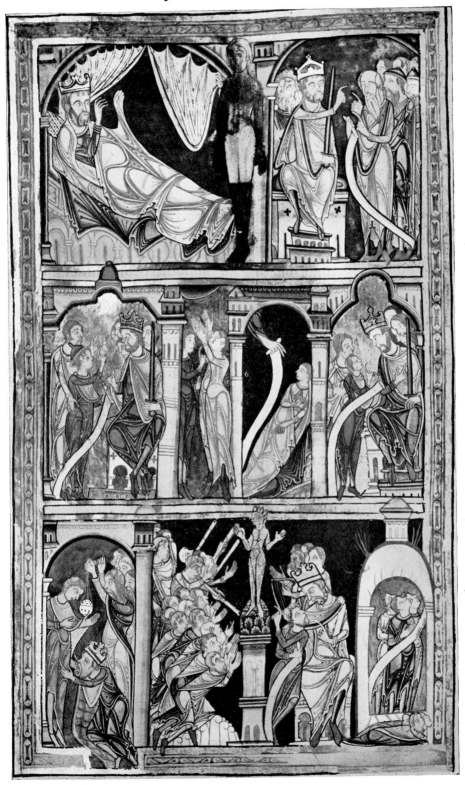

from the Lambeth Bible

But King Nebuchadnezzar forgot about the God of Daniel and made a golden image for a god and told everyone to worship it. When they heard the sound of a cornet, flute, harp, sackbut, psaltery and dulcimer, they were to fall down and worship it. There they are and Nebuchadnezzar looking on. But Daniel's three friends would not worship the idol, and the king was full of fury and cast them into a burning fiery furnace. The people who threw them in were killed (there they are lying in the flames below the furnace), but Shadrach, Meshach and Abednego walked in the midst of the fire unhurt, praising God. I expect you know the song they sang, 'All ye works of the Lord, bless ye the Lord, praise him and magnify him forever.'

XXVI

Shadrach, Meshach and Abednego were like the Christian martyrs; they were ready to die rather than worship false Gods. Daniel was like a martyr too. Twice he was thrown into a den of lions. This picture shows the second time, when he was left there six days. But God remembered him and sent him food. Far away in Judea, a prophet called Habakkuk had boiled pottage and broken bread in a bowl and was going into the field to carry it to the reapers. And the angel of the Lord said to him, 'Carry the dinner which thou hast into Babylon to Daniel who is in the lion's den.' He said, 'Lord, I never saw Babylon, nor do I know the den.' And the angel took him and carried him by the hair of his head and set him in Babylon. And Habakkuk cried saying, 'O Daniel, thou servant of God, take the dinner that God hath sent thee.' And Daniel said, 'Thou hast remembered me, O God, and thou hast not forsaken them that love thee.'

We have seen how the prophets foretold the coming of our Lord, and then the establishment of God's Kingdom on earth, the Church. Here is another prophet Joel foretelling how the Holy Ghost too was going to be sent to men. He is sitting, telling the people the wonderful and terrible things that God had told him to speak. 'And it shall come to pass after this that I will pour out my spirit upon all flesh; and your sons and your daughters shall prophesy: your old men shall dream dreams and your young men shall see visions. Moreover upon my servants and handmaids in those days I will pour forth my spirit.' On the day of Pentecost when the Holy Ghost came like a fire on to the apostles and they started to preach, St Peter cried out these same words, saying, 'This which was foretold by the prophet Joel, now it has come to pass!'

God looks after Daniel

from the Lambeth Bible

He speaks through Joel

from the Winchester Bible

And still it goes on happening; God pours out his Holy Spirit on us all, each one of us when we are baptised. When we are baptised we are marked too with the sign of the cross of Jesus, to show that we belong to him, and that it is through him our sins have been forgiven. That too was foretold in the Old Testament by the prophet Ezechiel.

XXVII

Ezechiel looked into heaven, and saw many visions. In one of them he saw Jerusalem—for he like Daniel had been carried into captivity and had to live in Babylon. 'And, behold six men came from the way of the higher gate, which lieth toward the north, and every man a slaughter weapon in his hand; and one man among them was clothed with linen, with a writer's inkhorn by his side:' God called to the man clothed with linen and said to him, 'Go through the midst of the city, through the midst of Jerusalem, and set a mark upon the foreheads of the men that sigh and that cry for all the abominations that be done in the midst thereof.' And to the others he said, 'Go ye after him through the city and smite, but come not near any man upon whom is the mark.' At the end the man clothed with linen returned saying, 'I have done as thou hast commanded me.'

The mark he put on their forehead was the last letter of the Hebrew alphabet, Thau. You see it is like a cross; St Jerome says the ancient way of writing it was as a cross. Who is it who marks their foreheads, who comes and goes so attentively to what God commands, who holds their heads and marks their foreheads so gently and carefully? Why, our Lord! The linen cloth wound round him is the pure body that he took from Our Lady. The inkhorn he has with him is for writing the book which he will carry when he comes at the end of the world (look at the Frontispiece); in it will be the names of the people he has marked and saved. The people who he marks are those who are sad because so many people are disobeying and forgetting him, thinking instead about the earthly city, not wanting the mark on their forehead which makes them Christians and lets them into the city of God. How wonderful to think that it is our Lord himself who puts his mark on our forehead!

from the Lambeth Bible

XXVIII

And now at last the time has come for which God made such careful preparations. It is time for him to fulfil his promise to Abraham, 'In thee shall all the nations of the earth be blessed.' Look, he is sitting in heaven, holding the world in his hand, telling the angel Gabriel to go to Our Lady; see how ready he is! I expect you know many pictures of the other end of the story, of Gabriel in Our Lady's house telling her, 'Behold thou shalt conceive in thy womb and shalt bear a son, and shalt call him Jesus. He shall be great, and men shall know him for the Son of the most High; the Lord God will give him the throne of his father David, and he shall reign over the house of Jacob eternally; his Kingdom shall never have an end.' And she said, 'Behold the handmaid of the Lord; let it be unto me according to thy word.'

God has decided to send his Son; mankind, through Our Lady, has freely accepted him. Now the ladder between heaven and earth can be made, God will become man, the Word we saw wrapped in the mysterious life of the Trinity will become flesh, will take a body, and be one of us. No wonder the angels sang and praised God when they told the shepherds. Now the prophecy that we saw pictured in the Tree of Jesse is going to come true, and 'mercy and truth have met one another, justice and peace have kissed'. God's mercy was longing to help man, to give him peace, to bring him to heaven, but his justice and his truth could not pretend that he did not know about man's wickedness and sin, that he was black and unfit to go to heaven, that none of the sacrifices, even of the good men, were enough to wash them clean. God became a man himself so that as a man he could take the punishment we all deserved. He came as a second Adam to lead us out of the bog into which we have followed the first Adam. We must hold on to him and then we shall be rescued.

God sends his son at last

from the Psalter belonging to the nun at Shaftesbury

XXIX

And here on the next page is one of the Evangelists, St John, ready to write the story of our Lord's life on earth—what he did and what he said, so that all the Christians who came after might know. He is looking up to God to ask him to make sure that all that he writes shall be true. There above him are the Trinity and all his angels round. All round the picture are people listening to what St John shall write; down the sides you see many kings, in the circles in the middle are the apostles, at the bottom, holy priests and monks, and in the middle do you see two angels holding a cloth and in it many, many people? That is you and me, the souls of all the people in the world listening to God's New Testament, the New Covenant God is going to make with men, to take the place of the Old one that he made with Moses.

Do you see that great eagle perched on St John's chair? He is one of the things Ezechiel saw in heaven. St John himself saw them too 'in the midst where the throne was, round the throne itself were four living figures, that had eyes everywhere to see before them and behind them. The first was that of a lion, the second that of an ox, the third had a man's look and the fourth was that of an eagle in flight'. They are the four evangelists, St Matthew, St Mark, St Luke, and St John. That is why the eagle is with St John.

In the New Testament which he and the other evangelists are going to write, the meaning of all the prophecies of the Old Testament are going to be made clear. Do you remember Pl. XXIV, how God is unveiling the face of the synagogue? Who is it on the other side who is being led forward crowned like a queen? Do you remember Pl. XII, how Hagar and Ishmael have to go into the wilderness to make room for Sarah, the free woman, and her son born by a miracle? God is coming now to make us free. Not just to rescue us from our sins (then we should still be his servants) but by a miracle to remake us so that we shall be his children, to invite us to be more than men, to share the very love of the Trinity (look at Pl. II) and to love one another with God's love. That is the commandment of the New Covenant, to love with God's love. How far beyond all we could have expected or deserved! St Augustine sings a great song to praise it. 'This is the love that shall renew us, make us new men, heirs of the New Testament, singers of the New Song. It is it which will renew the nations and from the universal race of men make and gather together a new people, the body of the newly-married bride of our Lord of whom it is said in the Song of Songs, "Who is she that ascendeth, made white?"' It is she who is being led forward, crowned like a Queen! She is the Church, the ark where we are safe (Pl. VIII), the mother who prays for

from the Grimbald Gospels

us (Pl. XVIII), the mountain which shall stand for ever (Pl. XXV). How is it she is all these things? Because she is the bride of Christ, the Virgin whom the unicorn loved (Pl. I), and that is why we belong to her, because she joins us to him.

XXX

Look where he comes to seek her! Look, he is rushing out of heaven to save us! Is that Gabriel, the angel who goes before him? Meeting him is the Psalmist; one of all those prophets who foretold his coming and proclaimed the message that God gave him, words which are now come true, 'for the words of the Lord are pure words, as silver tried in a furnace, purified seven times.' And below are all the people who have cried to God, all the poor and the ill-treated who have trusted in God. We too are there, for we have prayed to him to help us, all the people who are hungry for bread and those too who are hungry to know the truth—the people he is going to make into his Church. God is coming at last to help us. 'Now will I arise,' saith the Lord.

And look how he has come! Not as a great God, but as one of us, so little, so near us! How gentle and humble Our Lady looks, with God the Son in her arms, God the Holy Ghost over her head! I wonder if the Devil will recognise him? He will not expect God to come humbly like this. I expect that will catch him out!

The picture of God rushing out of heaven is an illustration to a psalm, from the same book as Pl. XXI. It is only part of the picture because as we saw before, different parts illustrate the different thoughts which follow one another in the psalm. You can see that the thoughts which the artist illustrates are not so much those of the poet who wrote the psalm, as of the Church which has taught us their secret, prophetic meaning. Both these drawings are by Anglo-Saxons; I expect you can tell which pictures are Anglo-Saxon by now. The Anglo-Saxons seem able to draw people so that their whole heart shows, in the way they stand, or stretch their hands, or turn their heads. But the artists are better, I notice, at drawing people who are loving, and confiding, and obedient, than those who are angry or disagreeable. Perhaps that is because they were more like that themselves? This Psalter is a copy of a very famous book called the Utrecht Psalter because it is now in Utrecht. But though it follows that book, which was written more than a century before in France, very closely, its drawings are very much alive, and very like the other Anglo-Saxon drawings. How different they are from the next pictures, which were made for a Norman bishop, the brother of King Stephen.

Our Lord comes rushing out of Heaven

from the Anglo-Saxon Psalm Picture Book

and becomes one of us

from the Service Book of the New Minster of Winchester

XXXI

This book is also a psalter but instead of illustrating the psalms themselves, it begins with a series of pictures illustrating the Old Testament from Adam and Eve (Pl. VII), and the life of our Lord. This one has fascinating pictures, but unfortunately someone has scraped the beautiful blue paint off the background (to use on their own pictures, I suppose; the paint was difficult to get). That is why the background is streaky.

God came to be an ordinary, poor child, but though he may not have wanted Satan to know him, he wanted all the people who were waiting for him or seeking him to recognise him. And so he told his angels to tell the shepherds in the fields, and so in a different way he told the wise men far away in the East. I expect that all their lives they had been seeking God, wanting to know the truth, like many other people who were not Israelites, and therefore did not know about the prophecies, or how God had shown himself to Abraham and Jacob and Moses and Elijah. So God showed at the very beginning that the New Covenant was for them too, for all of us. He showed them by a star. There they are on their horses at the beginning of their journey, pointing and telling one another about this wonderful new star which has appeared in the sky. A star! God suggests to us by the very sign he used what he was doing; he was giving a new light to men. When we are in the dark we cannot tell where we are or what we should do, everything is strange and unknown and we are lost, and then the light comes and we can see. The light which our Lord came to bring us, shows us everything, why we have been given life, and who gave it to us, and what we should do with our lives. At first the kings only saw the light in the distance. Straight away they left their earthly kingdoms to follow it, and it led them straight to Bethlehem. If we follow the light of the truth, it is sure to lead to God, and we shall find him, like his great star, wonderful and unexpected.

Look, they have arrived! Do you think that this was what they expected to find—a baby and his mother? But now they have found them, the kings know that this is what they really sought, and are glad beyond measure. They are presenting the gifts they have carried with them on their long journey. God must have suggested to them what they would need—gold to show that this poor baby was really a King, frankincense, like the incense we offer in Church, to show he was God, and myrrh to show that he was also really a man. God had planned it all from the beginning and even foretold the kings' journey and their gifts.

from the Psalter of Bishop Henry of Blois

XXXII

The kings had told Herod that they would visit him on their way home and tell him if they had found the new King. Here they are in their bedroom; I expect they are still in Bethlehem expecting to start their journey next day. It looks as if they all had to share a bed. You see they have hung up their crowns on the wall. They would not have minded being uncomfortable; they had found something far more important. There is God's angel come to visit them while they are asleep. He is telling them that they must not go back to Herod, but go home a different way. Herod was not like them, he did not seek the truth or love God, and so he will not be able to find the baby. But they must go home a new way; after we have found God, we have to live his new life.

There below is St Joseph in his bedroom. The angel has come to warn him, too, against Herod. 'Rise up, take with thee the child and his mother and flee to Egypt; there remain until I give thee word. For Herod will soon be making search for the child, to destroy him.' From the very beginning, it seems that there were people who hated our Lord, who did not want the promise to be fulfilled, who wanted the world to go on in their way, without God interfering. The people who wanted to belong to the earthly city did not want the City of God to come. You remember what Herod did? He killed all the babies in Bethlehem, hoping that he would kill this new King among them. But he could not catch God out. Joseph had already started on his long journey to Egypt and God looked after the other children too; they were the first people who died for our Lord. It is nice to think that they were children. God gave them all crowns. St John saw them in heaven; there, they follow our Lord wherever he goes.

from the Psalter of Bishop Henry of Blois

XXXIII

Here, St Joseph and Our Lady and Jesus are setting out on their journey to Egypt. They have just passed out of the gate of Bethlehem. Already Jesus is lifting up his hand to bless everyone they meet. I expect he blessed all the animals too in the desert as they journeyed through it. St Joseph is carrying their luggage on the end of his stick. They have not got much, but there is an angel with them to look after them.

When Herod was dead, you remember, they came back and lived in Nazareth, and our Lord lived and worked there among the people who lived there, just like one of them.

One day, St John the Baptist began to preach in the wilderness beyond the Jordan. Many people went to listen to him, and Jesus went too, and was baptised by John with the others, and 'suddently the heaven opened, and the Holy Spirit came down upon him in bodily form, like a dove, and a voice came from heaven, which said, "Thou art my beloved Son, in thee I am well pleased." ' Then St John knew him. God had told him that the purpose of his baptism was to make known to Israel the son of God, that he should know him, because God's Spirit would come down and rest upon him. St John was the last of the prophets; he was so great that his coming was prophesied by Isaiah; he was the one who was to 'straighten out the way of the Lord'. And now he pointed to our Lord so that everyone could see, 'Look, this is he who takes away the sins of the world.' This was he who God had taught them in so many ways, for so long, to expect. Now that he has come, God makes that quite clear, too. I think all those fishes in the Jordan round our Lord's feet must have known as well, without being told.

Why did our Lord choose to make himself known by being baptised? He had no need to be baptised because he had no sins to be washed away. He was showing us that baptism was his sign, that we must all be baptised; we must hold his hand and go with him and be baptised by one of his servants, and the Spirit will come on us too. Look at the lovely robe the angel is holding for us! We must try and keep it clean and beautiful all our lives, fit to wear at the feast in heaven when we die.

He has to fly to Egypt

from the Psalter of Bishop Henry of Blois

St John the Baptist prepares his way

from the Psalter of Bishop Henry of Blois

XXXIV

But the devil was frightened and angry. Who were these men calling people away from him to God? What was the meaning of these great signs, the star, the dove? Surely God could not really love men enough to become one of them—they who were so foolish and stupid, and proud because they did not even know about themselves, who lived through their bodies which tied them down to earth, which made them so easy to tempt and to hurt. He went to find out. He must fight our Lord if he wants to keep the power over men, which he won when he made Adam and Eve disobedient.

He found our Lord in the wilderness, when our Lord was hungry. Look, there he is trying to tempt him through the body Jesus has taken! 'If thou art the Son of God, bid this stone turn into a loaf of bread!' You can see the stones at their feet; our Lord would not touch them. Then Satan took him to Jerusalem and set him down on the pinnacle of the Temple. 'If thou art the Son of God, cast thyself down from this to the earth!' If Jesus were really a man, perhaps he would like God to do a special miracle for him in front of everyone, to show how good he was. But he refused to try. There, at the bottom, Satan has taken him to the top of a high mountain, and is showing him all the kingdoms and the riches of the world and offering them to him. Look at all the wonderful things—a crown and a royal drinking horn, gold rings and bowls and necklaces, sheep and oxen and horses. At the time when this picture was painted, these things meant all the wealth of the world because the rich people were those who owned gold and land, and cattle, rather than money. But the price of owning all this was to worship the devil. The devil knew that anyone who loves money and possessions is sure to forget about loving God; you cannot love two quite different things with all your heart.

The devil was beaten in that encounter. And Jesus was glad he came because he was able to show us how he understands, is with us, in all the different sorts of temptations which come to us, so that with him, we may learn how to beat the devil. Because he became a man, he himself was tempted with us, because we have become—by baptism into his Church—part of him, we, like him, with him, can win the victory.

from the Psalter of Bishop Henry of Blois

XXXV

Then our Lord began to preach and to call the people to follow him. Great crowds came to listen to him. One day he came to Jericho. There was a rich man there called Zaccheus who wanted to see what Jesus was like, but when he went out into the streets he could see nothing, for he was very small and could not see over the heads of the other people. So he ran on in front and climbed a tree. There is Zaccheus in the tree—he can see Jesus now, and behind are our Lord's disciples and the great crowd. 'Zaccheus, make haste and come down; I am to lodge to-day at thy house.' How lucky Zaccheus was! He had only hoped to look at Jesus and now he was coming to his house to spend the night with him. He came down with all haste and gladly made him welcome. When they got home, he said to Jesus, 'Here and now, Lord, I give half of what I have to the poor; and if I have wronged anyone in any way, I make restitution of it fourfold.' Outside the people were complaining; Zaccheus had not been a good man—you can guess from what he said that he had not made all his money very honestly. But Jesus answered them, 'That is what the Son of man has come for, to search out and save what was lost.' We were all lost in the dark forest of sin, only some people do not like to admit they are lost; the only pathway that leads out is our Lord, for he said, 'I am the way'.

Does Zaccheus' tree remind you of any other? Later, we shall read part of a wonderful poem about that other tree, the one Jesus climbed (Pl. XL). He said we must have a tree too, we must carry our cross, and this story tells us what happens if we do as he told us. We are usually in a crowd in our lives, lots of people round us asking us to join in many things, and they make it very difficult to see Jesus. So perhaps he shows us a tree, a pain or something disagreeable, or giving up something nice. If we climb it quickly, look, not only shall we see him suddenly but he will come to our house. We shall know he is very near us.

He teaches the people

from the Bury St Edmunds Gospels

XXXVI

Jesus taught the crowds who followed him by stories, just as God had taught the Israelites in the Old Testament by stories. This is one about the New Commandment he was giving, that we should love our neighbour as ourselves. Someone said, 'Who is my neighbour?' Our Lord told this story. 'A man who was on his way down to Jerusalem from Jericho fell in with robbers who stripped him and beat him and went off leaving him half dead.' There are the cruel robbers wounding him, and there he is lying by the roadside naked and bleeding. 'A priest saw him there, and passed by on the other side. And a Levite who came there saw him, and passed by on the other side. But a certain Samaritan who was on his travels, saw him and took pity at the sight; he went up to him and bound up his wounds, pouring oil and wine into them and so mounted him upon his own beast, and brought him to an inn where he took care of him.' Which of these proved a neighbour to the man who had fallen in with robbers?

But Jesus did not teach only in stories, but in his whole life. Was he not himself like the Good Samaritan? In the eyes of God it must have seemed, before Jesus came, as if all mankind were lying there by the roadside, tricked by the devil, wounded by his own sins, and because of them not able to move and help himself. Like the poor people in Pl. XXXA. God came; he poured the oil and wine of his grace and his sacrifice on the wounds, and bound them up, and then he lifted us on his ass (for all mankind means you and me, each one of us); look how he holds us carefully so that we shall not fall off the ass, and brings us to the inn. There we are looked after all our lives, for the inn is the Church. While we are still alive, we are travellers, making our journey through the world and we must live in it as in an inn, but when we die, in heaven, it will be our home.

from the Bury St Edmunds Gospels

XXXVII

As well as teaching people Our Lord proved before them that he was God by doing miracles. These are two pictures of miracles. One day after he had been teaching, he told his disciples to take a boat and cross the lake before him, and 'he went up by himself on to the hillside to pray there; twilight had come and he remained there alone. Meanwhile the ship was already half-way across the sea, hard put to it by the waves, for the wind was against them. And then when the night had reached its fourth quarter, Jesus came to them, walking on the sea. They were terrified and said, "It is an apparition," and cried out for fear. But all at once Jesus spoke to them: "Take courage," he said, "it is myself; do not be afraid." And Peter answered him, "Lord, if it is thyself, bid me come to thee over the water." He said, "Come," and Peter let himself down out of the ship and walked over the water to reach Jesus. Then seeing how strong the wind was, he lost courage and began to sink; whereupon he cried aloud, "Lord, save me." And Jesus at once stretched out his hand and caught hold of him.' The little boat on the water reminds us of the ark (Pl. VIII); they are safe in it because Our Lord is looking after it. He is looking after St Peter too. It is like walking on the water trying to live the new life Our Lord came to bring us. It seems impossible, and so it is without him, but he is there living with us; that is why we are able to do it, and he will catch hold of us too if we forget and begin to sink.

Below he is raising Lazarus from the dead. He is standing by the tomb, behind him are his disciples. On the other side are the sisters of Lazarus, Martha and Mary, and their friends. 'Jesus cried in a loud voice, "Come out Lazarus, to my side." ' See, the dead man has raised himself! 'He came out, his hands and feet tied with linen strips, and his face muffled in a veil.' That is the way the Jews wrapped up the bodies of dead people before they put them in a tomb. This was one of Our Lord's last and greatest miracles. Before he did it, he told its hidden meaning to Mary. He was going to raise the whole world from death, from lying buried in its sins, to life, to live forever with God. 'I am the resurrection and life, he who believes in me, though he is dead (for we must still die) will live on, and whoever has life and has faith in me to all eternity cannot die.'

from the Psalter at Glasgow

XXXVIII

But he did not come just to preach and teach and prove he was God, he came to make a great action, to finish the fight with the devil, to make the sacrifice. Now the time has come. It is the Passover, the time of the great sacrifice of the Israelites which God had taught them in Egypt. He told them then how they were to take a lamb and kill it and mark their doorposts with its blood, and then when God went through Egypt in the night killing the first-born of every house, those houses which were marked with blood he would pass by. That sacrifice of the Passover was a shadow to make people understand what is going to happen now. Our Lord came at the Passover because he was the Lamb. It is with his blood that people are going to be marked, as he is marking them on Pl. XXVII; then they will be saved.

Look, there he is coming on the ass the apostles found for him. There are the apostles following him carrying palms (like that palm on Pl. III) because he is coming to his great victory. Look at the people above pulling branches off the olive trees to throw at his feet. Olive branches, like the branch that the dove brought to the ark, to show the peace and mercy our Lord is going to bring to the world by his victory. He is just reaching the gate of Jerusalem; they are spreading their clothes under his feet because he is a King. On Palm Sunday the priest goes outside the Church and knocks on the closed door. That is because he is pretending to be our Lord. He knocks on the door because when Our Lord came to Jerusalem on that Palm Sunday he came to knock on the door of the New Jerusalem; knocking at the door of heaven, and we are all following in his train!

This picture is from one of the earliest and grandest of the Anglo-Saxon books, the Benedictional, or book of blessings for particular feast days, made for St Aethelwold. St Aethelwold lived in the middle of the tenth century when people in England had grown very worldly and had forgotten how much their ancestors, like Bede and Caedmon (*v.* p. 18), had tried to serve God. There was hardly a monastery in England lived in by monks. St Aethelwold and his friends St Dunstan and St Oswald tried to awaken people and many followed them and gave themselves to God by becoming monks. At Winchester, where St Aethelwold was bishop, monks came to live again in the ancient monasteries—the Old Minster and the New Minster. One of the ways in which they tried to praise God and teach people about him was by making pictures like this; this book says that St Aethelwold ordered that it might be made to help him to sanctify all his people, so that he might lose no lambkin of his fold. With the revival of the monasteries came a revival of the art of illustrating books. Many others of the pictures in this book

from the Service Book of St Aethelwold

were made at Winchester (Pls. XXXB and XLVII, and later Pls. XXVIB and XXXI-IV) and Pl. XL was perhaps made for St Oswald.

XXXIX

And now is the moment for which Jesus said he had longed and longed. Here he is at the Last Supper with all his apostles. There is St John in his arms, leaning against him. How close! But we can be as close too. That is just what our Lord is doing. He is giving the sacrifice that he is going to make next day to his followers, in such a way that it is given to us too. He is uniting them to himself before he dies, so that they shall have part in his death, and so that after his death they may be able to act it over and over again, till the end of the world. He is acting as a priest. He is offering to God his own body and blood, which were going to be sacrificed next day when he dies, and he is promising to his apostles that whenever they do the same thing he will turn the bread and wine they use into his body and blood so that their sacrifice shall become this sacrifice of his. And so we, living now, when we take part in the Mass and go to Holy Communion are as near to him as St John was then, and so are kept joined to him who is going to die on the cross, so that we can still be joined to him when he re-enters heaven. That is why in the Mass we call him Lamb of God and ask that by it we may be 'made partakers of his divinity who vouchsafed to become partakers of our humanity'.

In front in the picture is Judas. Our Lord is saying, 'It is the man to whom I give this piece of bread who is going to betray me.' He is warning Judas, trying even at the last moment to save him.

Below is the same room a few minutes before. Jesus is washing the feet of the apostles. That is St Peter in front, looking so worried, 'Lord, is it for thee to wash my feet? I will never let thee wash my feet.' But Jesus said, 'If I do not wash thee thou hast no companionship in me.' He told them another meaning too, when he had finished, 'If I have washed your feet, I who am the Master and Lord, you in your turn ought to wash each other's feet. I have a new commandment that I give you, that you are to love one another; that your love for one another is to be like the love I have borne you. That will be the mark by which men will know you.'

And look on the next page—we can see what his love was like. Now he has made the sacrifice; he has borne our sins and received the punishment they deserved and died so that we might get to heaven. This is an Anglo-Saxon

from the Bury St Edmunds Gospels

drawing, so I am going to tell you part of an Anglo-Saxon poem to go with it. The poet dreamt that he saw the very cross on which our Lord died, and that it spoke to him.

XL

*It was long since: they hewed me low
(But I remember!) in the forest-row.
  They plucked me from my rooted heart,
Strong enemies, and by base art
Mismade me in a shape of scorn
And bid me swing their knaves unborn!
On men's shoulders I rode at last
To a little hill. Foes made me fast.
Then I saw the Lord of man
Press on to climb me!
I dare not bend against command
Of the Lord, though I saw the land
Quiver and shudder in its clay.
I could throw down all his foes
But I hold fast.*

*Heroic, fair,
This young knight who was God made bare
His breast. He was ready then,
In the sight of many, to ransom men.
He climbed the gallows, and he gave
No second thought, being sure and brave.
I shuddered when he clutched me round;
Flinch I dare not or fall to ground:
I was raised a cross, and it was I
Who swung an Emperor gallows-high:
The Lord of Heaven;
I durst not bow.
They drove dark nails through my side,
Open wounds of malice that abide
To be seen upon me. I durst not spurn
Our foes mocking us with hate and scorn.*

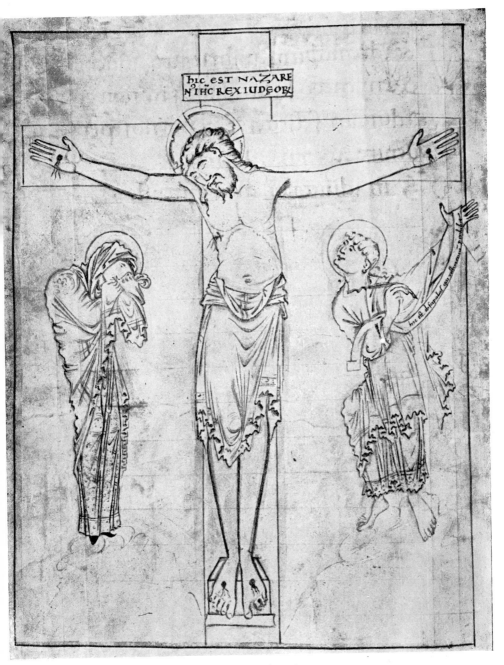

from St Oswald's Psalter

I was wet with blood fallen from the man's breast
When soul went out, a wavering guest.
On that little hill I have overlived and borne
Cruel deeds. I saw stretched out and torn
Woeful, the Lord of Hosts.

XLI

I think Our Lady looks as if she knowshe pain of all the people who suffer with Our Lord, because they love him. But St John is looking up. He is to bear witness to what Our Lord said, 'And I, if I be lifted up from the earth, will draw all things unto me.'

Darkness has masked the failing day,
Our Healer's body, bloodless clay
Stretched on the gallows, the weak rain
Wraps round and hides. This world of pain
With all creation, cries its loss.

He is dead. And now his soul goes down to Hell. To find all those who have died before him, who have loved him. He has come to rescue them. Look, there they stand at the mouth of Hell. Satan is chained. He cannot hold them. Our Lord has opened the great door; how lovingly he is bowing down and greeting them. There are Adam and Eve, Abel, I think, Sarah and Abraham, and many, many more. For St Matthew says how, when he died, 'the graves were opened, and many bodies arose out of them, bodies of holy men gone to their rest'.

Eve is speaking; it was through her that men fell into sin, but it is through her also that they have been saved, because our Lord was the son of her descendant, Mary. She is begging mercy for them all for Mary's sake. 'Lo! of my daughter wast thou born, O Lord, to help mankind on earth. Now is it seen that thou art God indeed, the everlasting source of all creation.' She need hardly beg, for now God's mercy is overflowing, for his justice and mercy kissed on the cross.

from an Anglo-Saxon Psalter in the British Museum

XLII

Look, he has won the victory! It is the night before the dawn of Easter day. The Church has written a wonderful hymn to praise that night. 'Exult now O hosts of angels in heaven! exult over the mysteries of God! Let the trumpet of salvation and acclamation sound for the victory of so great a King! Let the earth too, aglow with brightness, rejoice; let all men know that the darkness which overspread the whole world is chased away by the splendour of the eternal King. This is the night which even now all over the world lifts all those who believe in Christ out of the wickedness of the world, out of the darkness of sin, and gives them back grace, makes them partners in holiness. O happy sin of Adam which obtained for itself so dear and so great a Redeemer! O truly blessed night which alone deserved to know the time and hour when Christ rose again from hell, the night when heaven is united to earth, and God to man!'

Our Lord is standing on the devil; with his cross he has conquered him; in his hand is the book of life. Now at last our names may be written in it, if we have been marked too with the cross. The devil is shown as two creatures. He is a lion and a dragon. That is because he tries so many tricks—sometimes he is a lion raging around to see who he can devour, sometimes he is a dragon trying to catch by stealth. But he cannot catch us now anyway if we hold on to Jesus.

See, below the angels are holding great white sheets over us all, saying, 'Blessed are those whose transgression is forgiven, whose sins are covered.' Now at last God's justice is able to forgive us all, we are covered by the great sacrifice Jesus has made for us. We must get under that great sheet—that is why it is renewed for us every day in the Mass—or God will remember our sins, for nothing else can cover them up.

It reminds us of baptism, that great sheet. In the early Church when people were baptised they had to go right under the water, and act with their bodies what was happening to their souls. In the same way we have to get right under the sheet. But the sheet is our Lord's death on the cross; when we get under it we have to die with him, die to the devil and the old sin of Adam our father, and our own sins and bad habits, so that we can come out the other side new people, with God for our father, holding the hand of the second Adam, to live with him in the new free life of the light.

By his victory

from an Anglo-Saxon Psalter at Oxford

All our sins are covered

from the Anglo- Saxon Psalm Picture Book

XLIII

from the Anglo-Saxon Psalm Picture Book

But what has happened to his friends who had taken his dead body so sadly from the cross and put it in the tomb in the garden? Here are three of them—Mary Magdalene, Mary, the mother of St James, and Salome. They have come very early in the morning with spices to anoint his body. When they came to the tomb, they found an angel, his face shone like lightning and his garments were white as snow. He said to them, 'He is not here; he has risen, as he told you. You must go in haste and tell his disciples that he has risen from the dead; and now he is going on before you into Galilee.'

On the same day two disciples were walking to a village called Emmaus, near Jerusalem. They were talking very miserably of all that had happened, when Jesus joined them, but they did not recognise him. (They are all dressed as twelfth-century pilgrims, because if we are pilgrims, that is if we are trying to get to the city of God, we too may meet Jesus any day, though we may not know him.) They told him how Jesus had died, and how troubled they were, how the women went to the tomb and met an angel and found his body gone, but how none of them had seen Jesus again. He listened to them and then said, 'Too slow of wit, too dull of heart to believe all those sayings of the prophets! Was it not to be expected that Christ should undergo these sufferings and enter so into his glory?' He showed them how all the Old Testament prophecies had been fulfilled. They went into an inn together. When he took the bread and blessed and broke it, suddenly they knew who he was.

They went back to tell the others, but look, Jesus is with them already. There is St Thomas. St Thomas had said that he could not believe that Jesus was really alive again unless he could touch his wounds with his own hands. And a week later Jesus appeared in the room where they were and said to Thomas, 'Let me have thy finger; see, here are my hands. Let me have thy hand, put it into my side!' So because Thomas doubted, we can all know for sure that it was the same Jesus who died who came back to his disciples.

He comes back to his disciples

from the Bury St Edmunds Gospels

XLIV

But he did not stay with them long. Only for the forty days between Easter and Ascension day. One of the last things he did was to tell St Peter to look after us. He had taught them how they could think of himself as a shepherd, always guarding and feeding us, his sheep, and now he is handing the charge over to St Peter and saying to him, 'Feed my sheep.' Before he had said to him, 'Thou art Peter and upon this rock I will build my church; and the gates of hell shall not prevail against it, and I will give to thee the keys of the Kingdom of heaven.' Now he is giving him the keys, between them are the sheep, and above them the great edifice of the church. Look how carefully St Peter is looking after us. Look on Pl. XLVII. He has opened the door with his key and is welcoming us into heaven.

And now the forty days are over. He has just told his apostles that they are to go out and teach all nations about him to the ends of the earth. While he was speaking, they saw him lifted up, and a cloud caught him away from their sight. The two angels are saying, 'Men of Galilee, why do you stand here looking heavenwards? He who has been taken from you into heaven, this same Jesus, will come back in the same fashion, just as you have watched him going into heaven.' There in the Frontispiece he is coming back. Think of him coming to heaven! 'In the sight of all the angels, more glorious than any of them, a Man goes up to pass above all their ranks, higher than the archangels, on until he is received by God the Father, to sit with him on his throne, in glory.' 'Lift up your heads, O ye gates, lift them up ye everlasting doors; and the King of glory shall come in!' Isaiah saw him come to heaven. 'Who is this that cometh from Edom, with dyed garments from Bosra? this beautiful one in his robe, walking in the greatness of his strength?' 'I that speak justice and am a defender mighty to save!' 'Why then is thy apparel red and thy garments like theirs that tread in the winepress?' 'I have trodden the winepress alone; and of the Gentiles there is not a man with me.' Alone, he saved us; his garments are red with the blood of his victory.

The disciples rejoiced. They knew this did not mean that Jesus had left them. Indeed if he did not first go up to heaven, how could we follow him there? How can the angels go up and down the ladder if it is not partly in heaven? But it is only partly in heaven; there is still something else to happen.

He tells St Peter to look after us

from a manuscript of the Meditations of St Anselm

Then the first Man enters Heaven

from the Bury St Edmunds Gospels

XLV

He had told them to go to Jerusalem and to wait there. It is the fiftieth day since he rose from the dead. They are all together in an upper room, praying, and 'all at once a sound came from heaven, like that of a strong wind blowing, and filled the whole house where they were sitting. Then appeared to them what seemed to be tongues of fire (look, coming out from the Holy Ghost who has filled the room with his rushing), and they were filled with the Holy Ghost and began to speak in strange languages, as the Spirit gave utterance to each'. It has happened, what Jesus promised, that they should be baptised with the Holy Spirit. God the Son went back to heaven, so that God the Spirit should be with us, so that the whole Trinity should be with us. Now we know that we are invited, and able to love one another with God's own love, because the Spirit of his Love has come to live with us. Look how Love brings life; the apostles are like new men. The Holy Ghost has come upon them like a flame that shows that as well as making them burn with love, he is bringing a new light to their minds. Now they are able to speak all languages because they have to go out and teach all nations. Now the Church is alive! Our Lord joined them to him at the Last Supper, made them part of him, as it were, his body; now that body has been brought to life by the Holy Spirit. The Spirit has filled each one of them separately, but because it is the same Spirit that makes them all one. They are a new being, the Church—you remember how Our Lord came on earth to seek her, calling her his bride (Pl. XXX)? Now he and his bride are married. That is how the ladder is partly in heaven and partly on earth, how Our Lord is in heaven and yet still living with us till the end of the world. Because his bride (that is each one of us, together we make up the Church) is so dear to him, and so near to him that it is his own body, as Eve was part of Adam's body.

Or we can think again of the Church as the Ark. Now the dove has come back to it with the olive branch, Our Lord is Noah the steersman, and we are all inside. But we must not forget that the wood out of which the Ark is made is the wood of the cross.

The Birthday of the Church

from an Anglo-Saxon Psalter in the British Museum

XLVI

And so the Ark sails on through history from the day of Pentecost till the end of the world. And all the people in her have to try and live with the life of the Spirit and love the mark of the cross. Here is a story of St Peter and how he lived that life. Directly they had received the Spirit the apostles went about teaching everyone about Jesus, as he had told them to. But the Jews did not like this and St Peter was put in prison. You can see him looking out of the little window—he is chained inside. Outside is the guard. He has gone to sleep by the door, covering himself with his cloak and his shield. Suddenly an angel appeared to St Peter. 'Quick,' he said, 'rise up, throw thy cloak over thee and follow me.' Then St Peter's chains fell from his hands and he followed the angel. There they are going out of the prison gate; they have passed the guard; now they have reached the outer iron gate, which leads out into the city. It opens for them of its own accord. They came out, and as soon as they had passed up one street, the angel left him. God allowed him to be put in prison, but he sent his angel to look after him.

Later on when he was old, St Peter had a harder cross to climb, for he was crucified like our Lord, but then our Lord did not only come to his house (you remember the story of Zaccheus) but he brought St Peter to God's own house, the heavenly city, the new Jerusalem, to live with him for ever. And when we die we hope that he will bring us there too. Look over the page, there is St Peter at the door welcoming us and there are the guardian angels leading all the good people to the gate. St John the Evangelist saw the city; he says that it had a great wall and twelve gates, 'the building of the wall of it was of jasper, and the city was pure gold, like unto clear glass, and the foundations of the wall of the city were garnished with all manner of precious stones. The first foundation was jasper; the second, sapphire; the third, a chalcedony; the fourth, an emerald; the fifth, sardonyx; the sixth, sardius; the seventh, chrysolyte; the eighth, beryl; the ninth, a topaz; the tenth, a chrysoprasus; the eleventh, a jacinth; the twelfth, an amethyst. And the twelve gates were twelve pearls, and the street of the city was pure gold. And I saw no temple therein; for the Lord God Almighty and the Lamb are the temple of it. And the city had no need of the sun, neither of the moon, to shine in it, for the glory of God did lighten it, and the Lamb is the light thereof.'

from an eleventh-century music book

XLVII

But no one can go in whose name is not written in the book of Life of the Lamb, Our Lord. We must be very careful all our lives to think of the city of God and make sure we belong to it, to try to live the new life Jesus brought to us, of trying to be like him and loving everyone as he loves them. For look what happens to the people who only think of the earthly city, of getting what they want, and doing what they like, who forget about God and hate other people. The devil seems to have a book too and look, the angel is locking them all into Hell. But the devil cannot get a single one who loves God; look how St Peter is punching his nose with the great Key for trying to carry off a child who belongs to God.

from the Register of the New Minster of Winchester

XLVIII

When we die I hope our guardian angel will lead every one of us in turn up to that wonderful gateway. Look, here is a picture of St Michael carrying the souls of many people in his arms in a beautiful cloth. He is taking them up to Our Lord. I wonder if it is one of our souls in that sheet going up to meet God? I expect their guardian angels are waiting for them at the gate. The prayer book from which this picture comes was made for a nun who lived in a convent at Shaftesbury in the twelfth century. In it, opposite this picture, is a special prayer written for her in which she asks the archangel Michael to look after her soul when she dies and to carry it in his arms to heaven. I expect that he did not forget when the time came.

So we might end our book too with a special prayer, a prayer that we may follow the way about which the pictures have shown us so much.

Dear Jesus, please bless all the people who read this book, and all the people who made it and all the artists who drew the pictures. Please help us to live the New Life that you came to bring us, the life of loving everyone with your love, the love of the Holy Spirit who is living in us and trying to make us like you. Make us like you! That is how we can climb the ladder that leads to heaven. O Jesus, you are with us in the Ark which is going to carry us through our lives, you are steering it, so it cannot get lost. Help us to understand! Do not let us ever forget! You yourself have marked us with your cross, you have made us members of that city which lives with your life on earth. O bring us, please, to heaven where we may see that city with our eyes. Bring us to see you, so that we may be able really to thank you, and to love you with all our hearts.

from the Psalter belonging to the nun at Shaftesbury

List of Plates

FRONTISPIECE. THE SECOND COMING OF OUR LORD.

Devonshire Collection, Chatsworth Estates Company. Benedictional of St Aethelwold, f. 9v., $11\frac{1}{2} \times 8\frac{1}{2}$ ins., written at Winchester for St Aethelwold, bishop 963–984.

Tolhurst, 'An examination of two MSS. of the Winchester school. The Missal of Robert of Jumieges and the Benedictional of St Aethelwold,' *Archaeologia,* Vol. LXXXIII.

I. THE LEGEND OF THE UNICORN.

Bodleian Library, Oxford. Bestiary. Ashmole MS. 1511, f. 6v., $4\frac{1}{4} \times 4\frac{1}{2}$ ins. Late twelfth century. (Photograph, Oxford University Press.)

The source of the legend is obscure; it is quoted with varying interpretations, often the virgin is Our Lady. St Gregory quotes it (*Moralia*, Bk. XXXI, 29) with quite a different interpretation.

II. THE TRINITY.

British Museum. Psalter. Harley MS. 603, f. 1, unfinished pen drawing with green and some red wash. Original $9\frac{1}{2} \times 9\frac{1}{2}$ ins.; in the reproduction the blank edges have been cut; it represents the drawing $8\frac{1}{2} \times 7$ ins. About A.D. 1000. Probably from St Augustine's, Canterbury. (Photograph, British Museum.)

On the Iconography v. E. Kantorowicz. 'The Quinity of Winchester,' *Art Bulletin,* 1947, A. Heinmann. 'L'Iconographie de la Trinité,' *L'Art chrétien,* 1934. St Augustine, *De Trinitate.*

III. THE FALL OF LUCIFER.

Bodleian Library. The Caedmon MS. Junius XI, p. 3, drawing in coloured inks, $12\frac{3}{4} \times 7\frac{1}{2}$ ins. About A.D. 1000. Probably from Christ Church, Canterbury. (Photograph, Oxford University Press.)

Isaiah, 14. 12. Luke, 10. 18. *The Junius MS.,* ed. G. P. Krapp, 1931. Genesis, l. 12–290. The translation here given uses passages from both Genesis A and Genesis B. The representation of hell as the mouth of an animal is an English idea. The examples in this book are some of the very earliest known.

IV. THE CREATION OF LIGHT.

Bodleian Library. The Caedmon MS. Junius XI, p. 6, drawing in coloured inks, 7×6 ins. About A.D. 1000. Probably from Christ Church, Canterbury. (Photograph, Oxford University Press.)

The Junius MS., ed. G. P. Krapp, 1931, l. 78–134. Bede, *Ecclesiastical History,* Book IV, Ch. XXIV.

V. THE CREATION OF THE ANIMALS.

Bodleian Library. Bestiary. Ashmole MS. 1511, f. 6v., $5\frac{1}{2} \times 4$ ins. Late twelfth century. (Photograph, Oxford University Press.)

List of Plates

VI. THE CREATION OF EVE.

Bodleian Library. The Caedmon MS. Junius XI, p. 9, drawing in coloured inks with some colour, 8 × 7 ins. About A.D. 1000. Probably from Christ Church, Canterbury. (Photograph, Oxford University Press.)

Genesis, 2. Romans, 5. 14. Rev., 20. 12. A complete facsimile of the Caedmon MS. was published by I. Gollancz in 1927.

VII. THE EXPULSION OF ADAM AND EVE AND THE MURDER OF ABEL.

British Museum. Psalter. Cotton MS. Nero, C. IV, f. 2, $10\frac{3}{4} \times 6\frac{3}{4}$ ins. About 1150–60. From St Swithin's Priory, Winchester. Damaged, the ultramarine of the background has been scraped off. (Photograph, British Museum.)

The Junius MS., ed. G. P. Krapp, l. 397–452. Genesis, 3. 4.

VIII. THE ARK.

Bodleian Library. Caedmon MS. Junius XI, p. 66, drawing in coloured inks, $9 \times 7\frac{1}{2}$ ins. About A.D. 1000. Probably from Christ Church, Canterbury. (Photograph, Oxford University Press.)

Genesis, 6. 8. St Augustine, *City of God*, Bk. XV, 26. On St John, Tract. VI, 2.

IX. THE BUILDING OF THE TOWER OF BABEL.

British Museum. Aelfric's paraphrase of the Pentateuch and Joshua. Cotton MS. Claudius, B. IV, f. 19, $11\frac{1}{2} \times 8$ ins. Eleventh century. From St Augustine's, Canterbury. (Photograph, British Museum.)

Genesis, 11.

XA. ABRAHAM AND HIS FLOCKS IN EGYPT.

British Museum. Aelfric's paraphrase of the Pentateuch and Joshua. Cotton MS. Claudius, B. IV, f. 22v., drawing in coloured inks with some colour, $3\frac{1}{4} \times 6\frac{3}{4}$ ins. Eleventh century. From St Augustine's, Canterbury.

Genesis, 12.

XB. ABRAHAM AND MELCHISEDEK.

British Museum. Prudentius. Psychomachia. Cotton MS. Cleopatra, C, VIII, f. 2v., drawing in red and brown inks, $2\frac{1}{2} \times 3\frac{1}{2}$ ins. Early eleventh century. (Photograph, Courtauld Institute.)

Genesis, 14–18. Hebrews, 7.

XIA. ABRAHAM AND THE THREE ANGELS.

Lambeth Palace Library. The Lambeth Bible MS. 3, f. 6. The upper half of a full page miniature, $8\frac{3}{4} \times 5\frac{1}{2}$ ins. First half twelfth century. (Photograph, Mr O. Fein, Warburg Institute.)

Genesis, 18. St Augustine, *City of God*, Bk. XVI, 31.

[110]

List of Plates

register of a full page miniature, frontispiece to Numbers, $3\frac{1}{2} \times 9$ ins. First half twelfth century. (Photograph, Mr O. Fein, Warburg Institute.)

Numbers, 4.

XVI. ILLUSTRATION TO PSALM 134 (A.V. 135).

Trinity College, Cambridge. The Canterbury Psalter. MS. R. 17. 1, f. 240, drawing in coloured inks, c. 7×12 ins. Middle twelfth century. Written at Christ Church, Canterbury.

It seems probable that the artist intended the incidents in the background to be typical only, not particular events or people.

XVII. THE STORY OF RUTH.

Lambeth Palace Library. The Lambeth Bible. MS. 3, f. 130. Frontispiece to the Book of Ruth, 5×9 ins. First half twelfth century. (Photograph, Mr O. Fein, Warburg Institute.

XVIIIA. THE PRAYER OF HANNAH.

Corpus Christi College, Cambridge. The Bury St Edmunds Bible. MS. 2, f. 146. Details of frontispiece to I Kings, $5 \times 1\frac{1}{2}$ ins. Illuminated by Master Hugo at the Abbey of Bury St Edmunds. (Photograph, Courtauld Institute.)

I Kings (I Samuel), 1. 2. St Augustine, *City of God*, Bk. XVII, 4.

XVIIIB. THE DEATH OF SAUL.

Lambeth Palace Library. The Lambeth Bible. MS. 3, f. 151. Upper part of initial F, $6\frac{1}{2} \times 5\frac{1}{2}$ ins. First half twelfth century. (Photograph, Mr O. Fein, Warburg Institute.)

I Kings (I Samuel), 15. 31.

XIX. DAVID AND GOLIATH.

Corpus Christi College, Cambridge. The Dover Bible. MS. 3, f. 116v. Initial at the beginning of I Kings, top and bottom of the same initial F, both 4×3 ins. Twelfth century. Written at St Martin's Priory, Dover. (Photograph, Courtauld Institute.)

I Kings (I Samuel), 17. St Augustine, *Sermons on N. T.*, CIII. 11. *Commentary on Psalms*, Ps. CXLIV.

XX. DAVID THE PSALMIST AS KING AND SHEPHERD.

Corpus Christi College, Cambridge. The Dover Bible, Vol. II, MS. 4, f. 13. Initial B at the beginning of the Book of Psalms. Twelfth century. Written at St Martin's Priory, Dover. (Photograph, Courtauld Institute.)

I Kings (I Samuel), 21. 24. II, 6.

XXI. ILLUSTRATION TO PSALM 103 (104).

British Museum. Psalter. Harley MS. 603, f. 51v., drawing in coloured inks, 5×10 ins. About A.D. 1000. Probably from St Augustine's, Canterbury. (Photograph, British Museum.)

The translation quoted is that of Mgr Knox of the new Roman Psalter. The text in the MS. is that of St Jerome's Roman Psalter.

XXII. ILLUSTRATION TO PSALM 30 (31).

British Museum. Psalter. Harley MS. 603, f. 17v., marginal drawing in coloured inks, $3 \times 6\frac{1}{2}$ ins. About A.D. 1000. Probably from St Augustine's, Canterbury. (Photograph, British Museum.)

Ps. 30 (31), 21 (22).

XXIII. ELIJAH TAKEN UP TO HEAVEN IN THE FIERY CHARIOT.

Corpus Christi College, Cambridge. Dover Bible, Vol. I, MS. 3, f. 161v. Initial at the beginning of IV Kings, $13\frac{1}{2} \times 5$ ins. Twelfth century. Written at St Martin's Priory, Dover. (Photograph, Courtauld Institute.)

IV Kings (II Kings), 2. III Kings (I Kings), 19.

XXIV. THE TREE OF JESSE.

Lambeth Palace Library. The Lambeth Bible. MS. 3, f. 198, $15\frac{1}{2} \times 11$ ins. First half twelfth century. (Photograph, Mr O. Fein, Warburg Institute.)

Isaiah, 11. Ps. 74 (75). A. Watson, *The Early Iconography of the Tree of Jesse*, 1934.

XXV. THE DREAM OF NEBUCHADNEZZAR, AND THE THREE CHILDREN IN THE FIERY FURNACE.

Lambeth Palace Library. Lambeth Bible. MS. 3, f. 285. Frontispiece to the Book of Daniel, $14\frac{2}{5} \times 8\frac{4}{5}$ ins. First half twelfth century. (Photograph, Mr O. Fein, Warburg Institute.)

Daniel, 2. 3.

XXVIA. DANIEL IN THE LION'S DEN.

Lambeth Palace Library. Lambeth Bible. MS. 3, f. 286. Initial A at the beginning of the Book of Daniel, $5\frac{1}{2} \times 6$ ins. First half twelfth century. (Photograph, Mr O. Fein, Warburg Institute.)

Daniel, 14. (Apocrypha, Bel and the Dragon).

XXVIB. THE PROPHET JOEL.

Winchester Cathedral Library. The Winchester Bible, f. 200v. Late twelfth century. From St Swithin's, Winchester. (Photograph, Victoria and Albert Museum.)

Joel, 2. 28. Acts, 2. 16.

XXVII. THE MAN CLOTHED IN LINEN WITH A WRITER'S INKHORN.

Lambeth Palace Library. Lambeth Bible. MS. 3, f. 258. Frontispiece to

Ezechiel. Details, $4\frac{1}{2} \times 1\frac{8}{10}$ ins., $4\frac{1}{2} \times 2$ ins. (Photograph, Mr O. Fein, Warburg Institute.)

Ezechiel, 9. St Jerome, *Comm. in Ezechielem*, Lib. III, 10. St Gregory, *Moralia*, Bk. XXII, 18.

XXVIII. GOD ENTHRONED, WITH THE ANGEL GABRIEL.

British Museum. Psalter. Landsdowne MS. 383, f. 12v., 7×4 ins. Somewhat before mid twelfth century. Written for a nun of St Edward's Abbey, Shaftesbury. (Photograph, British Museum.)

M. A. Farley and F. Wormald, 'Three related Romanesque MSS.', *Art Bulletin*, 1940.

XXIX. ST JOHN THE EVANGELIST.

British Museum. Gospels. Add MS. 34890, f. 114v., $10 \times 9\frac{1}{2}$ ins. Early eleventh century. Probably from New Minster, Winchester. Called the Grimbald Gospels because it contains a copy of a letter to King Alfred about a French scholar and monk, Grimbald. Grimbald came to England more than a century before this MS. was written. (Photograph, British Museum.)

St Augustine, *On St John*, Tract. LXV, 1. Ezechiel, 1. Apocalypse, 5.

XXXA. CHRIST COMING TO THE HELP OF HIS PEOPLE.

British Museum. Psalter. Harley MS. 603, f. 6v. Detail, parts of figures illustrating other ideas in the psalm which abut on this subject have been painted out in order to square up the picture. About A.D. 1000. Probably from St Augustine's, Canterbury. (Photograph, Courtauld Institute.)

A reproduction of the whole page is given in O. E. Saunders, *English Illumination*, I, Pl. 30. A facsimile of the Utrecht Psalter has been published by E. de Wald, 1932.

XXXB. VIRGIN AND CHILD.

British Museum. Church Offices. Cotton MS. Titus, D. XXVII, f. 75. Detail, drawing in red and brown inks with touches of colour, $2\frac{1}{2} \times 1$ ins. About 1012–20. From New Minster, Winchester. (Photograph, British Museum.)

XXXI. THE JOURNEY AND THE ADORATION OF THE MAGI.

British Museum. Psalter. Cotton MS. Nero, C. IV, f. 12, $10\frac{3}{4} \times 7$ ins. About 1150–60. From St Swithin's Priory, Winchester. (Photograph, British Museum.)

St Leo, Sermon XXXVI. Matthew, 2. Ps. 71 (72). Isaiah, 60.

XXXII. THE DREAM OF THE MAGI AND OF ST JOSEPH.

British Museum. Psalter. Cotton MS. Nero, C. IV, f. 13, 11×7 ins. About 1150–60. From St Swithin's Priory, Winchester. (Photograph, British Museum.)

Matthew, 2. Apocalypse, 14. 4.

List of Plates

XXXIIIA. THE FLIGHT INTO EGYPT.

British Museum. Psalter. Cotton MS. Nero, C. IVA, f. 14, $6 \times 7\frac{1}{4}$ ins. About 1150–60. From St Swithin's Priory, Winchester.

XXXIIIB. THE BAPTISM OF OUR LORD.

British Museum. Psalter. Cotton MS. Nero, C. IVA, f. 16, $5\frac{1}{2} \times 7$ ins. About 1150–60. From St Swithin's Priory, Winchester.

St Augustine, *On St John*, Tract. IV. St John, 1.

XXXIV. THE TEMPTATION.

British Museum. Psalter. Nero, C. IV, f. 18, 12×7 ins. About 1150–00. From St Swithin's Priory, Winchester. (Photograph, British Museum.)

Luke, 4. St Leo, Sermon XXII, 4. St Augustine, *On St John*, Tract. II. 14 *On Psalm LXI* (A.V.), 3.

XXXV. THE CALLING OF ZACCHEUS.

Pembroke College, Cambridge. Gospels. MS. 120, f. 2. Ink drawing, heightened with colour, c. 8×8 ins. Early twelfth century. From Bury St Edmunds Abbey. (Photograph, Victoria and Albert Museum.)

Luke, 19. St Augustine, *Sermons on the N. T., CXXIV*.

XXXVI. THE PARABLE OF THE GOOD SAMARITAN.

Pembroke College, Cambridge. Gospels. MS. 120, f. 2. Ink drawing, heightened with colour. The upper half of the same page as XXXV, $4\frac{1}{2} \times 8$ ins. Early twelfth century. From Bury St Edmunds Abbey. (Photograph, Victoria and Albert Museum.)

Luke, 10. St Augustine, *Sermons on the N. T., CXXI*.

XXXVIIA. JESUS ON THE SEA SAVING ST PETER.

Hunterian Museum Library, Glasgow. Psalter. MS. 229 (U. 3. 2), Q. 4, f. 1v. Lower half of full page miniature, $4\frac{1}{4} \times 5\frac{5}{8}$ ins. (Photograph, Glasgow University.)

This subject occurs on the same page as a representation of *St Thomas resolving his Doubt*; the previous page has the *Journey to Emmaus*, and the succeeding, *The Ascension*, which would suggest that this page is an illustration to John 21, though the treatment seems to correspond better to the incident of our Lord walking on the water.

Matthew 14. St. Augustine, *Sermons on N.T., XXVI*.

XXXVIIB. THE RAISING OF LAZARUS.

Hunterian Museum Library, Glasgow. Psalter. MS. 229 (U. 3. 2), Q. 3, f. 1v. Lower half of full page miniature, $3\frac{7}{8} \times 4\frac{3}{4}$ ins. Late twelfth century. From the diocese of York. (Photograph, Glasgow University.)

John, 11. St Augustine, *On St John*, Tract. XLIX.

XXXVIII. Christ entering Jerusalem.

Devonshire Collection. Chatsworth Estates Company. Benedictional of St Aethelwold, f. 45v.; in the reproduction the edges of the border have been cut. Size of whole page, $11\frac{1}{2} \times 8\frac{1}{2}$ ins. (Photograph, Victoria and Albert Museum.)

Roman Missal, Blessing of the Palms.

XXXIX. The Last Supper: Christ washing the Feet of the Apostles.

Pembroke College, Cambridge. Gospels. MS. 120, f. 3, c. 8×8 ins. Early twelfth century. From Bury St Edmunds Abbey. (Photograph, Courtauld Institute.)

Luke, 22. Roman Missal, Offertory and Canon of Mass. John, 13.

XL. Crucifixion.

British Museum. Psalter. Harley MS. 2904, f. 3v., drawing in coloured inks, as shown (the page is larger), 10×8 ins. Written at Ramsey Abbey between 974 and 986. (Photograph, Courtauld Institute.)

C. Niver, 'The Psalter in the British Museum, Harley 2904,' in *Medieval Studies in Memory of A. Kingsley Porter*, 1939. It is suggested here that this may be the Psalter of St Oswald, the founder of Ramsey Abbey. 'The Dream of the Rood,' trans. Gavin Bone, *Anglo-Saxon Poetry*, 1943. John, 12.

XLI. The Harrowing of Hell.

British Museum. Psalter. Cotton MS. Tiberius, C. VI, f. 14, drawing in coloured inks, 10×6 ins. Damaged at the edges. About 1050. (Photograph, British Museum.)

'The Dream of the Road.' Christ and Satan (*Junius MS.*, ed. Krapp), l. 435.

XLIIa. Christ Victorious. Illustration to Ps. 90 (A.V. 91). Conculcabis leonem et draconem.

Bodleian Library, Oxford. Psalter. Douce MS. 296, f. 40, drawing in coloured ink, heightened with colour; the elaborate border of the original has been omitted. Early eleventh century. From Crowland, Lincolnshire. (Photograph, Oxford University Press.)

Extract from the *Exultet*, Holy Saturday, Morning Office, Roman Missal. St Augustine, *Commentary on Ps. 91* (A.V.).

XLIIb. Illustration to Ps. 31 (A.V. 32), Beati Quorum tecta sunt peccata.

British Museum. Psalter. Harley MS. 603, f. 18. Detail, drawing in coloured inks, $4\frac{1}{5} \times 10$ ins. About A.D. 1000. Probably from St Augustine's, Canterbury. (Photograph, Courtauld Institute.)

Romans, 6.

List of Plates

XLIIIa. THE THREE MARIES AT THE TOMB.

British Museum. Psalter. Harley MS. 603, f. 8. Detail from illustration to Ps. 15 (A.V. 16), drawing in coloured inks, $3 \times 3\frac{4}{5}$ ins. About A.D. 1000. Probably from St Augustine's, Canterbury. (Photograph, Courtauld Institute.)

Matthew, 28.

XLIIIb. THE PILGRIMS TO EMMAUS.

Pembroke College, Cambridge. Gospels. MS. 120, f. 4v., drawing in sepia, $8\frac{1}{2} \times 8$ ins. Early twelfth century. From Bury St Edmunds Abbey. (Photograph, Courtauld Institute.)

Luke, 24. John, 19.

XLIVa. CHRIST GIVING THE KEYS TO ST PETER.

Bodleian Library, Oxford. Psalter and Meditations of St Anselm. MS. Auct., D. 2. 6, f. 169, 3×3 ins. Twelfth century. (Photograph, Courtauld Institute.)

John, 21. Matthew, 16.

XLIVb. THE ASCENSION.

Pembroke College, Cambridge. Gospels. MS. 120, f. 5v., drawing in sepia, $6\frac{1}{2} \times 8$ ins. Early twelfth century. From Bury St Edmunds Abbey. (Photograph, Courtauld Institute.)

Acts, 1. St Leo, Sermon LXXIII, 4. Ps. 23 (A.V. 24). Isaiah, 63. 1.

XLV. THE DESCENT OF THE HOLY GHOST.

British Museum. Psalter. Cotton MS. Tiberius, C. VI, f. 15v., drawing in coloured inks, $8\frac{1}{2} \times 5$ ins. Damaged at the edges. About 1050. (Photograph, British Museum.)

Acts, 1. St Gregory, *Homily 30 in Evang.* St Augustine, *Sermons on N. T.*, XLI, 7. I Corinthians, 12.

XLVI. ST PETER RELEASED FROM PRISON.

British Museum. Troper (liturgical book with musical notations). Cotton MS. Caligula, A. XIV, f. 22. Eleventh century. Possibly from Hereford. (Photograph, British Museum.)

Acts, 12. Apocalypse, 21.

XLVII. ST PETER AT THE DOOR OF HEAVEN.

British Museum. Register and Martyrology of New Minster, Winchester. Stowe MS. 944, f. 6v. and 7, drawing in coloured inks with some colour, $8\frac{3}{4} \times 5\frac{1}{2}$ ins. Written at Winchester about 1016–20. (Photograph, British Museum.)

XLVIII. ST MICHAEL CARRYING SOULS TO HEAVEN.
British Museum. Psalter. Lansdowne MS. 383, f. 168v., $7 \times 4\frac{1}{2}$ ins. Somewhat before mid-twelfth century. Written for a nun of St Edward's Abbey, Shaftesbury.